SIXTY Y

To Roy,

My time as a fan of Crystal Palace Football Club

Best wishes,

Martin Jones

Feb 2026

MARTIN JONES

Published in the United Kingdom 2025

by Martin Jones

ISBN 978-0-9935522-5-0

Printed by Johnsons Printers

Front Cover – the 'Fab Four' - left to right, Philip Odell, the author, Andrew Williams and Martin Everett at Selhurst Park in 2009.

Special Note from the author

All proceeds from sales of this book will be donated to the Palace for Life Foundation and MIND in Croydon for their work in the local communities.

CONTENTS

ACKNOWLEDGEMENTS

As with my previous books, much of the material for this book comes from my own personal memories and archives. Nevertheless, there are a number of people I would like to thank for their contributions, in particular:

Ian King, club historian at Crystal Palace Football Club, who was the author of the book, *Crystal Palace, The Complete Record, 1905 – 2011*, and who readily agreed to allow me to use material from his book in support of my book.

My good friend, Martin Everett, for supplying me with some very useful archive material from our early days at the Palace, which I have been able to use in this book.

My brother Colin, sister-in-law Mary and their family for allowing me to use their photos of the 2025 FA Cup Final and Victory Parade in this book, and my friend Andy Everett for the same reasons.

Gayle H and John T from the Rate the Ref website who provided me with supporting information.

My wife Marta for (once again) agreeing to read through the various drafts and making encouraging comments and suggested amendments.

And not forgetting my longstanding friends and Palace fans, Martin Everett, Philip Odell and Andy Williams. Between us, we have racked up over 250 years of supporting Crystal Palace, and I am pleased that I have been able to recognise this in a small way by getting us all on the front cover of this book, and elsewhere in the book. Thank you chaps!

I am grateful to you all and to anyone else who has contributed but whose name I have inadvertently overlooked.

INTRODUCTION

When I became a pensioner a few years back, I decided it was time to record and publish some memories of my life and support charitable causes in the process. This is the sixth book in the series and covers my support for Crystal Palace Football Club since the early 1960s. And lest it be thought that I was about to impart secret information about royalty, given the title of the book, let me confirm that it is Crystal Palace rather than Buckingham Palace, although the late Queen Elizabeth does get a mention in a roundabout way later in the book!

I have tried to avoid making this book a chronological account of games I have attended, that would be far too boring and long-winded, but rather a focus on games with a 'wow' factor – good or bad - which I hope may interest you, the reader. And whether you support 'South London's No 1' yourself, or Millwall, Charlton, Fulham, Brighton or any other club, I hope you will enjoy reading about my memories and perhaps rekindle some memories of your own. I invite you to read on.

The author, suitably attired, in 2015

HOW IT ALL BEGAN

It was 2.30pm on a bright April day in 1962 when I first lined up outside the Whitehorse Lane end of Selhurst Park - 1/9d (about 8p) - in my hand, to see Crystal Palace play in the Football League Division 3. If I was a bit apprehensive at what I would find inside, I should not have been since, as a twelve-year-old, I had already attended a number of games with my dad at Craven Cottage, White Hart Lane and even Wembley. However, this was the first time I had been to a league match on my own and the first time I had been to the Palace, so what would I find inside, and would I enjoy it and want to come back for more?

The key to my venture to Selhurst Park in 1962 was my dad, Trevor, who had been a football fan from an early age. Dad was brought up in Stockton-on-Tees and was a Middlesbrough fan, and he recalled being involved in a serious incident at a packed Ayresome Park in 1926 when barriers collapsed and several children at the front were injured, and my dad ended up on the pitch as the fans were tended and dispersed. Dad moved south during the Great Depression of the 1930s, and although he never returned north to live, he continued to support the Boro for the rest of his life, and I recall attending Ayresome Park on several occasions when we were on holiday close to my grandparents' home.

My interest in football also began from an early age, when accompanying dad to Civil Service matches in which he played as a robust full back, and in games at my local preparatory school and in back gardens with my friends. The interest really took off when my family accompanied dad to RAF Changi in Singapore for three years in the late 1950s and I played for my primary school, not as a robust full back, but as an outside left with a No 11 on my back. As a natural right-footer, I often wondered why I was selected for a position on the left of the attack, and after I was dropped from the team, I never returned to playing in that position. It was about this time that dad took me to see the national Singapore team play in a Cup match at a packed and rickety stadium in the city, and I was captivated by a world-class performance from the goalkeeper, a Eurasian by the name of Wilf Skinner, which enabled the home side to win the match and Cup 2-1. Henceforth, this 10-year-old wanted to be a goalie!

RAF Changi Primary School 2nd XI 1959/60, with me in the front row on the right.

If I had aspirations, they were quickly dashed on our return home to Surrey and my first sight of grammar school and the rugby pitches on the playing fields. It was clear from the start that football was not going to be an option at this school, and indeed the headmaster hated football so much that he banned footballs and anything resembling footballs from the school premises. This might have been a problem for the many boys who had been used to playing with the round ball at primary school, but very quickly, a group of us went out of the school at lunchtimes and played football on the local green. We played there for several years and the friendships we made have continued to this day, and in the case of Martin and Philip, they have included regular trips to see our favourite football team at Selhurst Park and elsewhere around the country. It is perhaps strangely ironic that a past Chairman of Crystal Palace is also an Old Boy of the school, although it has to be said that his time there came a lot later than mine and football was by then at least tolerated at the school.

Our love of football led a group of us to form a football team in the mid-1960s. Bradmore Green was the name given to the team after the green where we had first played in our lunch-hours, but soon we changed the name to Holmesdale United, reflecting our love of Crystal Palace and the end where several of us stood on a Saturday afternoon. After playing friendly matches for a while, we joined the Croydon Sunday League, with a pitch at often windswept Purley Way and changing facilities at the old outdoor pool nearby. By then, I had achieved my dream of playing in goal, but I was never likely to emulate my hero Wilf Skinner and, after enduring some cold, wet and draughty afternoons at Purley Way, I decided to call it a day.

Bradmore Green line up to play Woodcote Secondary School in 1965. I am the goalie on the right in the front row, and my good friend Martin Everett is fourth from the right in the same row. Other team members are Dave Patterson, Malcolm Wright, Nigel Aslin, Andrew Eustace, Roger Cox, Roger Everitt, John Lee, Nigel Pattinson, Denis Berridge and Chris Lock.

What next? Well, I had long had an interest in seeing the different referees in action at Selhurst Park and, in the late 1960s, I decided to take up the whistle. I passed my exam, purchased the required black uniform and a couple of metal 'Acme Thunderer' whistles, and prepared to do battle with players, some of whom I had previously known from my playing days. I also joined the Croydon Referees Society at their premises at the old Liberal Club, and for many years after, I enjoyed attending and participating in their monthly meetings, which included meeting refereeing celebrities such as Sir Stanley Rous and FA Cup Final referees, Ken Burns and Ron Challis.

A smart turnout of Croydon referees at a 6-a-side tournament in 1969, left to right, Seymour Procter, Graham Lumsden, Me, and Howard Manley.

On the field, I began refereeing in local leagues, including the Surrey Intermediate League and Croydon Sunday League. By the early 1970s, it seemed that I was a bit of a 'blue-eyed boy' so far as refereeing was concerned, and by the time I was 23, I was a class 1 referee, the same class as refereeing legends such as Jack Taylor and Norman Burtenshaw. Being class 1, I refereed on the Surrey Senior League and Met London leagues and 'lined' on the Isthmian League. It was on the latter league that I met up with aspiring and past Football League referees such as John Martin from Alton and formerly a Croydon colleague, Dennis Hedges from Oxford, John Homewood from Sunbury and Tony Oliver from Leigh-on-Sea, and what smashing blokes they turned out to be. I aspired to follow them, but a barrier quickly became evident and that was work. At the time, I was working away from home a great deal and this, coupled with commuting to and from London, meant that I could not devote the time to maintain the standards of fitness necessary to progress, and in 1978, I dropped out of the system 'by mutual consent', I think the term is. I know I was not the only one in this difficult position.

I was disappointed but determined to continue my refereeing in local leagues and in schools and youth football. I particularly liked officiating in schools football as this meant, as a class 1 referee, periodic visits to Football League grounds to officiate in English Schools trophy matches, and visits to Highbury (Arsenal), Goldstone Ground (Brighton), Plough Lane (Wimbledon) and the Priestfield Stadium (Gillingham) come to mind. However, all this ended when I moved north in 1989 and my days on the football pitches of London, Surrey and elsewhere in the Southeast came to an end.

I officiated at Selhurst Park just once, a friendly between Crystal Palace and near-neighbours Croydon Amateurs when I was a linesman and the referee was John Martin. I was due to referee the Croydon Primary Schools Final there in the late 1980s, but heavy rain on the morning of the game put paid to that and I was not involved when the match was re-scheduled.

I have digressed and now return to April 1962 and my first visit to a ground which was to become a second home for me over the next sixty years.

GAMES WITH A ‘WOW’ FACTOR!

Game 1 – CPFC v Bournemouth, 23rd April 1962, Division 3

I am sure my first game at the Palace needs to be included in this book despite the lack of an obvious ‘wow’ factor.

In keeping with other League grounds, the Selhurst Park I first encountered in 1962 was ‘basic’ to say the least, with facilities to match. There was standing room on all four sides, with only the upper part of the Main Stand having seating where my friends Martin (and his dad) and Philip had season tickets for many years. And only the Main Stand provided cover against the elements, so not perhaps a ground to enjoy on a cold, wet winter’s day. One highlight of each home game which I recall to this day was the lady who toured the ground announcing ‘roasted peanuts, sixpence a bag’ in a loud, shrill voice. I do not think I ever partook of her wares, and I knew nothing about her background until recently when a match-day programme confirmed that she had been a grandma of six with a wonderful history. I wish I had known more about her at the time, but this was not something I was ever likely to ask her about as she passed by.

I had already heard that the Palace teams of the early 1960s were free-scoring, with 110 League goals in season 1960/61 and over 80 goals prior to the match v Bournemouth and, as the away side were looking for promotion to Division 2, with over 80 League goals to their credit already, it seemed that we could be in for some goals and entertainment during the afternoon. However, there was a ‘fly in the ointment’, in that the Palace had sold their high-scoring forward Johnny Byrne the previous month to West Ham United for a then record British transfer fee of £65,000, and the goals had dried up thereafter. As an example, the game against Bournemouth was played on Easter Monday and Palace had drawn a blank two days previously when the corresponding fixture was played at Bournemouth (Easter fixtures against the same side being a norm in those days), so the signs were not promising.

I remember little about the game. I know I stayed at the Whitehorse Lane end throughout and did not join the many youngsters who used to scoot from one end of the ground to the other to ensure they were behind the goal that Palace were attacking. As it was, there were no goals for the youngsters to cheer at the Holmesdale Road end in the first half, and I was joined at half time by many of them anxious to see the net bulging at the Whitehorse Lane end in the second.

Did we see any goals? Well, it was not for want of trying, but as the clock ticked down to ninety minutes, we were still waiting. Then, at last, the perfect cross came in and there was Palace forward Dennis Uphill diving full-length to head the ball into what seemed to be an empty net. Alas, he got it all wrong and the ball crashed against the crossbar and back into play. The game ended soon after, goalless, and the smallish crowd dispersed disappointed.

Was I disappointed? Yes. Did I go back for more? Well, I think you know the answer to that already.

Amazingly, 63 years after the game, my friend Martin has produced a team-sheet from the game, and this is set out below, along with a picture from an annual of Johnny Byrne in his early days at Selhurst Park. More on Johnny later. Funny how little that part of the ground has changed over the years.

Result CPFC 0 Bournemouth 0, attendance (rounded) 11,300, referee Ken Burns

Postscript

As a former referee, I have included the names of the referees for most of the games in this book including this one.

Bournemouth did not get promoted that season and lest I be accused by a current friend of not calling them by their correct name – AFC Bournemouth – this did not happen until 1971 and in fact the club was named 'Bournemouth & Boscombe Athletic' in the early 1960s. But 'Bournemouth', I am sure, will suffice on this occasion.

EXCLUSIVE!

RONNIE ALLEN writes for the

CROYDON TIMES

SERIES

BE RIGHT ON THE BALL AND TAKE THE "TIMES"

CRYSTAL PALACE Colours: White with Claret and Blue Facings Black Shorts

Vic Rouse

2 Johnnie McNichol — 3 Roy Little

4 Terry Long — 5 Brian Wood — 6 Eddie Werge

7 Ron Brett — 8 Roy Summersby — 9 Dennis Uphill — 10 Andy Smillie — 11 Ron Heckman

Referee : K. H. Burns (Worcs.)

Kick-Off 3.0 p.m.

CROYDON TIMES

Linesmen : W. Webster (Red Flag) J. W. Wilkes (Yellow Flag)

11 Bennett — 10 Archer — 9 Dowsett — 8 Weller — 7 Spelman

6 Bolton — 5 Nelson — 4 McGarry

3 Jones — 2 Farmer

Best

BOURNEMOUTH Colours : Red and White Shirts White Shorts

CRYSTAL PALACE FOOTBALL CLUB

Match reports appear every week in

THE STREATHAM NEWS - PENGE & ANERLEY NEWS

THE NORWOOD NEWS - NORBURY & THORNTON HEATH NEWS

ON SALE EVERY FRIDAY Price 4d.

DINGWALL MOTOR

Game 2 - CPFC v Mansfield, 24th Nov 1962, FA Cup 2nd Round

If my first game at Selhurst Park had ended goalless and with no real 'wow' factor, the second certainly did not.

Mansfield were the opponents in the 2nd round of the FA Cup in season 1962/3, Palace having eased through the 1st round 2-0 against non-League Hereford at Selhurst Park. At the time, Mansfield were in Division 4, a division below Palace, but they were already heading for promotion by late November and, with Palace in the doldrums with only two league wins to their name in Division 3, a close game seemed likely.

I do not recall the pattern of scoring, but I do know that Peter Burridge scored the very first Palace goal I ever saw in my sixty years as a fan. However, as the clock ticked into the ninetieth minute, Mansfield were leading 2-1 and seemingly on their way to dumping the home side out of the FA Cup. Then, drama at the Holmesdale Road end as a Palace player went down in a heap and the referee pointed to the penalty spot. Bedlam ensued as the Palace fans roared their approval and the disapproving Mansfield players surrounded the referee. I was at the Whitehorse Lane end again and could not really see the incident, but it was clear the Mansfield players were far from happy at the award. No problem though for Palace veteran Ronnie Allen, who had scored a vital penalty for West Bromwich Albion in the 1954 FA Cup Final, and the Palace were level at 2-2.

With the final whistle coming almost immediately after, that might have been it, but the Mansfield players were still clearly very unhappy and some unsavoury scenes seemed to ensue at the entrance to the players' tunnel which was located at the time by the halfway line under the Main Stand. I thought nothing more of it, but shortly after, it was reported that ten Mansfield players had been 'booked' by the referee (no yellow cards in those days) for sarcastically applauding him off the pitch. The exception was apparently the goalkeeper who failed to make it to the tunnel entrance in time to join in.

I often wondered how true the report was, but just recently, my attention was drawn to a newspaper report (below) confirming that the referee had indeed booked the ten players. The referee was named as Kevin Howley - like Ken Burns in Game 1 an FA Cup Final referee - and the report went on to suggest that the players concerned were 'severely censured and warned as to their future conduct'.

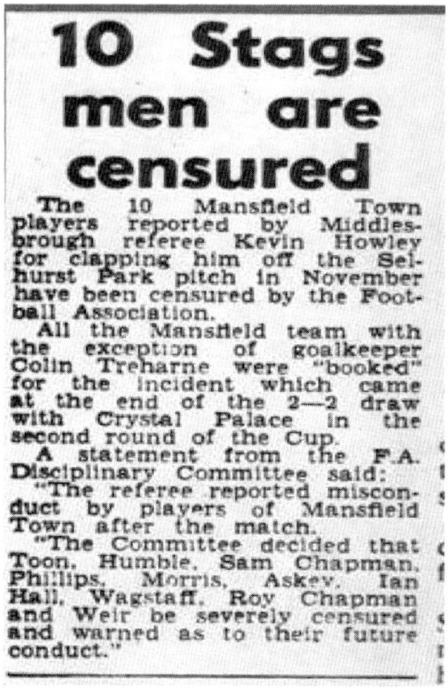

10 Stags men are censured

The 10 Mansfield Town players reported by Middlesbrough referee Kevin Howley for clapping him off the Selhurst Park pitch in November have been censured by the Football Association.

All the Mansfield team with the exception of goalkeeper Colin Treharne were "booked" for the incident which came at the end of the 2—2 draw with Crystal Palace in the second round of the Cup.

A statement from the F.A. Disciplinary Committee said: "The referee reported misconduct by players of Mansfield Town after the match.

"The Committee decided that Toon, Humble, Sam Chapman, Phillips, Morris, Askey, Ian Hall, Wagstaff, Roy Chapman and Weir be severely censured and warned as to their future conduct."

Need Mansfield have bothered? No, as it turned out, they crushed Palace 7-2 in the replay just 48 hours later, and with Kevin Howley in charge again.

Result CPFC 2 Mansfield 2, attendance 13,400, referee Kevin Howley

Postscript

The poor early-season form and FA Cup exit cost Palace manager Arthur Rowe his job. He had been manager since April 1960 and had guided them to promotion from Division 4 in his first full season with the club. But now he made way for Dick Graham and thereafter the Palace steadily climbed the table to finish a respectable half-way, and the signs were promising for the following season.

I was not to see another game at Selhurst Park until Easter Saturday, 13th April 1963, when I saw Palace score twice in the last five minutes to win an exciting game against Bristol City, 3-2. My absence might have seemed a bit surprising, except that the winter of 1962/3 was one of the coldest and snowiest of the twentieth century, and in fact Palace failed to play any home games between 26th December 1962 and 16th March 1963 because of the weather, with the backlog of games not finally cleared until the end of the extended season on 22nd May. Such were the vagaries of winters in those days of long ago.

The front cover of a programme from my early days at Selhurst Park

Game 3 – CPFC v Oldham, 25th April 1964, League Division 3

The signs were indeed promising and, after a disastrous start, 1-5 at Coventry, Palace steadily climbed the table, including no defeats between the start of January and 11th April 1964. By the beginning of April, they had every chance, not only of gaining promotion but of winning the division, with only Coventry City barring their way. Sadly for the Palace, their good form then deserted them, and five draws and a disastrous home defeat to lowly Barnsley meant that they had to win or draw their final game of the season against Oldham to finish top and hope that Coventry dropped points at home to Colchester.

Of course, I had to be there and, for the first and only time in his life, my dad decided to come along as well. I would have been quite content to stand for two hours, but my dad had other ideas and we managed to secure two seats in what was called the Wing Stand on the edge of the Main Stand.

All went well in the first half and when Palace legend Cliff Holton gave the home side the lead from the penalty spot, it seemed the party could begin on the packed terraces, with toilet rolls festooning the goal areas and touchlines, and it did not seem to matter at half time that Coventry were also leading 1-0. Sadly, an Oldham forward named Ledger had other ideas and his hat-trick in the second half meant that Palace were relying on Colchester to equalise at Coventry. And, as the half progressed and it became obvious that Palace were going to lose, the fans began to anxiously listen on their 'trannies', not only to hear how Coventry were getting on, but also Watford who could snatch the second and final promotion spot from the Palace with a win at Luton, no play-offs in those days. At the final whistle, the fans surged on to the field and stood in front of the Directors' Box to await the results from elsewhere. And then they came through - Coventry 1 Colchester 0 and Luton 2 Watford 1 - and the party could well and truly get underway. Palace may not have been Champions of Division 3, but they were now promoted and could look forward to life in Division 2 for the first time.

It took a while for the players to appear in the box, but nobody was bothered. The party on and off the pitch seemed to go on forever and it was approaching 6pm by the time my dad and I finally exited the stadium and headed home. My dad was not into emotions, and I cannot recall how he felt about his one and only visit to Selhurst Park, but I do know that I was one very happy teenager.

Result CPFC 1 Oldham 3, attendance 28,000, referee Roy Harper

Postscript

Just recently, I was reading a media account of an 8-year-old boy who attended the Palace v Oldham game with his dad, and his dad took some cine film of the game. Amazingly, the footage now appears on YouTube, and I have thus been able to enjoy reliving the game from over sixty years ago. Footage of toilet roll paper festooning the goalmouth at the Holmesdale Road end and being cleared by a linesman from the touchline reminded me of a practice which has long died out in English football (thank goodness); and a clip of fans streaming onto the pitch at the end of the game and the later scenes of the players in the Directors' box brought back many happy memories. I thoroughly recommend a view of the film.

Game 4 - CPFC v Nottingham Forest, 20th February 1965, FA Cup 5th Round

Palace's first season in Division 2 started off badly, with a 2-3 home defeat to Derby in August 1964, a game which I saw. However, after losing the first three games, Palace put together seven wins in eight games and minds began to turn to promotion to the 'big time'. However, that was as good as it got, and by the following February, they were having a solid if unspectacular season in Division 2 under the guidance of Dick Graham.

Thoughts turned to the FA Cup where of course for the first time, Palace were not required to participate until the 3rd round. Bury were brushed aside in that round, but Southampton away in round 4 proved to be sterner opposition, with Palace emerging creditable 2-1 winners from a match which was amazingly played on the same day as Winston Churchill's national funeral was taking place in London. Needless to say, I stayed at home to watch the funeral with all its pomp and ceremony.

At the time, the draw for each round was made at 12.30pm on the following Monday and broadcast only on BBC radio, and being a schoolboy at the time, I must have relied on a 'tranny' at lunchtime to hear the draw for the 5th round. And so I heard, 'Crystal Palace will play at home to Nottingham Forest', and with Forest flying high in Division 1, this was a game which I had to attend.

It was the custom in those days for cash to be paid on entry to the ground at the turnstiles, no online booking or credit cards around then, and because a record crowd of over 40,000 was expected for the game, I arrived early, so early that I actually saw the gates being opened at 12noon. Even so, there was quite a queue to go in and it was 12.30pm before I made my way on to the open terraces, having ensured that I visited the rudimentary toilet facilities first, no newspapers on the ground for emergency use during a long afternoon, as was apparently the custom on the terraces at Anfield! It was a cold, damp, winter's afternoon and I must have been chilled to the bone standing there for over two hours before the clock ticked down towards 3pm and kick off time, with only the warmth from the growing number of fans on either side to stop me from freezing over altogether.

At last, the familiar sounds of 'Glad All Over' by The Dave Clark Five resounded over the loudspeakers and the Palace team emerged from the tunnel to roars of 'Yes I'm ...(stamp stamp)… glad all over' from the mass of fans on the terraces and we were ready for action. As suggested beforehand by manager Dick Graham, it quickly became clear that Palace were not there to make up the numbers and, as the game progressed and with the score 1-1, thanks to a Dave Burnside goal, thoughts must have turned to a possible upset. And then, midway through the second half, the perfect cross came over from the Palace left and there was Palace favourite Peter Burridge to volley the ball left-footed from the edge of the penalty area. Ninety-nine times out of a hundred, the ball would have ended up somewhere along the Whitehorse Road, but this was the hundredth occasion and the ball crashed into the top corner of the net, with the Forest goalkeeper rooted to the spot. The packed terraces went wild and I was actually glad that I was near the front. Now the fight was on as Forest sought to preserve their place in the FA Cup for another season, but that of course left them open to counterattack, and it was perhaps fitting that the final goal of the afternoon was scored by Palace legend Cliff Holton. The final whistle brought scenes of joy on the pitch and the crowded terraces. Palace were through to the 6th round and who would they play next?

I emerged from the ground some five hours after I had entered it, chilled yes, but totally ecstatic, like most of the fans around me. There was however more to come as the Palace game was on the fledgling Match of the Day that evening, the first time they had appeared on the programme. Just one camera situated towards the base of the Main Stand, grainy black & white pictures, no replays of goals and incidents and definitely no VAR, but I thoroughly enjoyed watching the proceedings, in particular Peter Burridge's volley. If ever there was a contender for 'goal-of-the-century' for the Palace, this was it.

Result CPFC 3 Nottingham Forest 1, attendance 41,700 (ground record), referee Ken Dagnall

The teams from that historic day in February 1965

CRYSTAL PALACE
(White)

1. John JACKSON
2. Bert HOWE
3. Terry LONG
4. John HOLSGROVE
5. Alan STEPHENSON
6. Peter BURRIDGE
7. Brian WHITEHOUSE
8. Roy HOROBIN
9. Cliff HOLTON
10. Keith SMITH
11. Bobby KELLARD

KICK-OFF
3.00 p.m.

Referee :
K. DAGNAL
Bolton

Linesmen :
J. E. WITTS
Swindon
(Orange Flag)

C. T. HOMEWOOD
Maidstone
(Cerise Flag)

NOTTINGHAM F.
(Red)

1. **Peter GRUMMITT**
Signed pro in May 1960. Played for England under 23's. Debut for Forest at 18 and a former ground staff boy.

2. **Peter HINDLEY**
Signed pro in June 1961. Previously a Forest amateur. League debut March 1963 v. Everton.

3. **Denis MOCHAN**
Signed from Raith Rovers in June 1962. Previously with East Fife. League debut January 1963.

4. **Henry NEWTON**
Born Nottingham. Joined ground staff Jan. 1960 and signed pro one year later. League debut October 1963.

5. **Robert McKINLAY**
Previously a Forest amateur. Signed pro July 1949. Member of 1959 Cup winning team. Almost 500 senior appearances. Longest serving player. Captain.

6. **Jeffrey WHITEFOOT**
Schoolboy and under 23 International. Previously with Manchester United and Grimsby. Another member of the 1959 Cup winning eleven.

7. **Ian STOREY-MOORE**
Signed amateur August, 1961 and pro in May 1962. League debut in, May 1963.

8. **Colin ADDISON**
Born Taunton and signed from York City Jan. 1961. League debut one week later.

9. **Frank WIGNALL**
Signed from Everton in June 1963. International cap. Also represented the Football League.

10. **John BARNWELL**
Signed from Arsenal in March 1964. England under 23 Cap. Previously Bishop Auckland.

11. **Alan HINTON**
Transferred from Wolves in Jan. 1964. Under 23 International also Full Cap.

Postscript

On 15 November 2023, Crystal Palace celebrated sixty years of playing 'Glad All Over' by The Dave Clark Five at home games. Unlike the present, it was only played when the Palace team first emerged from the tunnel, separately from the away team and officials in those days. In the early days, I recall it was alternated with another long-forgotten song, but by 1968, when the Five apparently played it live before a game at Selhurst Park, 'Glad All Over' had become the sole Palace favourite. I wonder how many times it has resounded around Selhurst Park over the past sixty years and how much in the way of royalties the band has received!

Game 5 - CPFC v Leeds United, 10th March 1965, FA Cup 6th Round

The 'trannies' must have been at work again the following Monday lunchtime, as news quickly got around at school that Palace had been drawn at home again, this time to mighty Leeds United.

This was another game I had to attend. However, a drawback quickly became evident as the authorities decided that the bulk of the tickets would be sold at Selhurst Park on a Sunday morning in advance of the game, and with another record crowd expected, it soon became clear that there would be an unprecedented demand on the appointed day to get tickets. In my case, there was only one thing for it, say a prayer that my absence from church would go unnoticed, check the tyres and lights on my trusty bike, and set my alarm for 4am with the aim of getting to Selhurst Park well in advance of the time the ticket windows were due to open.

Croydon was a strangely empty and eerie place to be cycling through before dawn on a Sunday morning, but I quickly negotiated the High Street and was pleased that traffic levels did not appear to be building up until shortly before I arrived at the ground. Perhaps my decision to get there early would pay off. However, this feeling quickly turned to concern as I arrived at the ground to see a queue of people already snaking back from the club offices up the road and around the corner to …. who knows where. There was only one thing for it, find a suitable place to park the bike and walk to the end of the queue. This turned out to be three-quarters of the way round the ground on the hill in Holmesdale Road, and with the time at 5am, it was clear that a long wait lay in store to get my prized ticket.

I have always been a bit of an 'early bird', but queuing at a football ground from two hours before dawn on a cold February morning was certainly not among my preferred activities for that time of day. The smell of Woodbines and Senior Service wafted through the air, coughing and spluttering was widespread, along with the shuffling of feet as thousands of fans struggled to keep warm. I recall some enterprising food and hot drink sellers did good business as they toured the queue selling their wares at greatly inflated prices, but I resisted the urge to buy a packet of roasted peanuts or maybe I did not have the money to buy this delicacy.

Eventually the birds began to sing and dawn broke to reveal the queue now stretching back to the start point, with the ground encircled with fans. I only hoped that the local constabulary would be on hand to keep the back of the queue away from the front when the windows finally opened.

The ticket windows were due to open at 9am, but when the hour eventually came and went, any thoughts that we would quickly move forwards were dashed, and it was to be another hour before we finally said farewell to the empty turnstiles in Holmesdale Road and shuffled up the hill and around the corner. Like me five hours before, people were still coming towards us trying to find the end of the queue in the distance, and I thought with grim satisfaction that they had no chance of getting a ticket. On and on we went until eventually the ticket windows – all two of them – came in sight and the nightmare would at last become a dream. And then, just feet from the prize …. BANG …. the windows slammed shut and the 'Sold Out' signs went up. The dream had been shattered and I would not be attending the game against Leeds United. It was 1pm.

Did we argue, did we swear, did we riot, did we storm the gates? No, we did not, instead we just shuffled away from the ground that had been our home for eight hours and prepared to head home, in my case sadly on my bike back through the by-now busy streets of Croydon.

Need I have been so upset? Probably not, as the game was first postponed because of heavy snow and then Palace succumbed rather too easily on the following Tuesday evening to a Leeds side who went on to contest the FA Cup Final against Liverpool.

So where was the 'wow' factor in a game which I did not actually attend? Well, there was one, but it was to be another fifty years before I became aware of it and, if I may, I will leave the details until later.

Result CPFC 0 Leeds United 3, attendance 45,400 (ground record), referee Jim Finney.

The front cover of the match-day programme in 1965 was a very plain black-and-white affair compared with earlier and later years

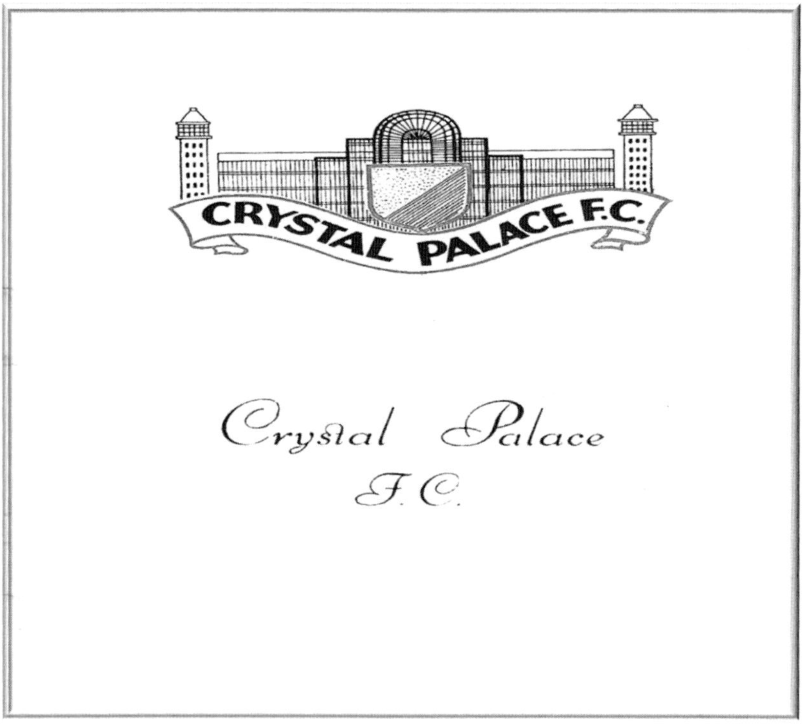

Game 6 - CPFC v Walsall, 31st January 1968, FA Cup 3rd Round

You may have noticed that I have fast-forwarded three years for my next game. This is not to say that nothing happened in the interim, only that I have not spotted any games with a 'wow' factor in them for me.

Dick Graham left the club in January 1966 and, after Arthur Rowe had acted as a caretaker manager for three months, Bert Head became manager from April 1966, having previously been manager of Bury. Bert was undoubtedly a great influence at the club, but not perhaps in his first two seasons when Palace remained around mid-table in Division 2. In the FA Cup, a long two-night trip by coach to Carlisle for my friends ended in disappointment as Palace slumped to a 0-3 defeat, and the score was the same the following season when any hopes of gaining revenge over Leeds United were quickly dispelled at Elland Road.

In February 1967, Bert brought Johnny Byrne back to the club, and whilst it soon became clear that the best days of the England international were past, it was hoped that he would bring some experience to the forward line, as well as a return to some of the goal-scoring feats of his earlier days at Selhurst Park. At the time of his arrival back, I was the manager of a local Cub football team and, to our great surprise, Johnny turned up one evening at a Pack meeting wanting his son Kevin to join the Cubs and play football. "When can he start?" we probably asked, and from then on, Johnny, who lived down the road from the park, regularly attended matches on a Saturday morning to watch his son play, much to the wonderment of the opposing players and, on one occasion, he even came on as a second half substitute when two teams of leaders played each other on a Sunday morning. But that is another story!

So we move forward to January 1968 and the third round of the FA Cup. A routine 1-1 draw at Walsall had us reaching for our 'trannies' again on the following Monday lunchtime, and to our delight, Palace or Walsall were drawn at home to mighty Liverpool in the fourth round, and with Walsall in a lower division, the omens were good as over 27,000 fans crowded into Selhurst Park for the replay.

Walsall may have been in a lower division, but they quickly dispelled any thoughts that they would easily succumb in front of a partisan crowd, and when they took the lead midway through the first half, it was thoroughly deserved. The second half saw Palace attacking with more and more intensity, but it seemed that they wanted to walk the ball into the net, and chance after chance went begging. Then, finally, with ten minutes remaining, Johnny Byrne (of course it had to be Johnny) equalised from close range, cue bedlam on the terraces and a sense of relief that all would be well, even if it took extra time to grind out a result. However, Walsall had other ideas and immediately went down the other end to score a cracking goal past Palace legend John Jackson. You could hear a pin drop and the silence continued long after the referee's whistle confirmed that it would be Walsall playing Liverpool in the 4th round rather than Palace. Our cup dreams were over for another year!

Result CPFC 1 Walsall 2, attendance 27,400, referee Vernon Batty

Postscript

Walsall held Liverpool to a 0-0 draw in the 4th round in a game where there were several injuries after a terrace wall collapsed. For Palace, the end of the season could not come soon enough, with just four wins in Division 2 between Christmas 1967 and May 1968, and it is one of these games that provides my final 'wow' factor of that forgettable season.

Game 7 - CPFC v Norwich, 16th April 1968, League Division 2

Easter 1968 saw Palace entertaining Norwich in back-to-back fixtures on consecutive days. This may seem strange now when there are automatic breaks of at least 72 hours between fixtures, but it was still the norm in those days of long ago. The game at Carrow Road on Easter Monday had been lost 1-2, and with Palace firmly rooted in midtable and without a win to their name since the first week of March, it was perhaps unsurprising that only 7,700 fans turned up for the return fixture at Selhurst Park the evening after, surely one of the lowest attendances I have witnessed at Selhurst Park for a first team League or Cup game. Would the fans who stayed away come to regret their decision? We were about to find out.

Remarkably, Palace took an early lead and the relief on the players' faces must have been palpable. And then they scored another… and another… and another. Goals rained in past the hapless Norwich keeper such that, as the game moved towards a conclusion, Palace were leading 5-0 and looking for more, with two goals each from Woodruff and Vansittart and the other from Danny Light. Would they get another? Step forward Mark Lazarus, a Palace player for only a few months, but already a favourite on the terraces and with a nickname reflecting his roots which could certainly not be published in this book. Mark's party trick, when he scored, was to run right round the pitch receiving the acclaim of the fans as he went. And so it came to pass that evening, with Mark scoring Palace's sixth and final goal from close range and immediately setting off on a lap of honour around the pitch with the fans roaring their approval from the terraces. Nowadays, Mark would probably have picked up a yellow card for time-wasting, but it did not seem to matter in those days and the Norwich players were clearly too shell-shocked to protest. I think we may have shouted for Mark to do a second lap, but either sense prevailed or he was too exhausted to do any more running and the game ended shortly after with Palace 6-0 winners, one of only two occasions when I have seen Palace score six in a

League game. It was a night to remember and, unlike the Walsall game, a night to remember for all the right reasons.

Result CPFC 6 Norwich 0, attendance 7,700, referee Derek Nippard

Palace favourite, Mark Lazarus, was famous for his laps of honour

Game 8 – Millwall v CPFC, 23rd November 1968, Division 2

Despite the mediocre season in 1967/8, the Palace board stuck with Bert Head as manager, and ambitious plans were passed to put a roof on the terraces opposite the Main Stand, to be known as the Arthur Wait Stand after the Palace Chairman. It remained to be seen whether the ambitions would be matched on the field in season 1968/9.

The early signs were promising, with three straight wins at the start of the season. However, that was followed by five games without a win including a 1-0 Friday night defeat at Fulham which my friends and I saw, when the winning goal was scored by big-money signing Frank Large following a horrendous mistake in the Palace midfield. Things then settled down and three straight wins set up a potential 'corker' against South London rivals Millwall at The Den.

In those days, Millwall were the arch-rivals to Palace rather than Brighton, and fixtures between the two sides were always eagerly awaited. Games at The Den (the old ground rather than the current one) were not for the faint-hearted and, with both teams looking for promotion and absolutely no segregation on the terraces, it was with some trepidation that my friend Philip and I made our way on to the packed terraces for the first fixture of the season between the two sides.

I think it is fair to say that the game quickly developed into a war of attrition, not helped by some extremely lenient refereeing. Palace were undoubtedly the main beneficiaries of this leniency, and when a Millwall favourite was carried off after a particularly bad challenge, the mood on the terraces started to become ugly, with chanting about kicking a few heads in following the game. This might not have mattered so much if Millwall had been leading, but by then, Palace had opened up a 2-0 lead, thanks to goals from Woodruff and Lazarus. With five minutes remaining and Philip and I moving towards the exit for a quick getaway, a Millwall player went down in the penalty area and the referee pointed to the spot. Back in the game? Not a bit of it as Palace goalie John Jackson dived to his right to produce a magnificent save. It was definitely time to go, and I think Philip and I were already on the train home when the referee blew the final whistle to confirm Palace as potential candidates for promotion.

Result Millwall 0 CPFC 2, attendance 27,900, referee Leo Callaghan

Another Palace favourite, Bobby Woodruff, measures up to be the long-throw champion of England 1968/9 (c/o Football League Review)

Game 9 – CPFC v Blackpool, 28th December 1968, Division 2

Christmas 1968 proved to be a 'White Christmas', with a mixture of wet snow and slush, interspersed with bright sunshine, making for a very seasonal Christmas Day in the local area. Strangely, Palace had to travel all the way to Sheffield United for the Boxing Day game and returned home with a creditable 1-1 draw to keep their promotion hopes alive. Two days later, the snow had largely cleared, but it was still freezing cold as close on 19,000 of us headed to Selhurst Park for a League game against Blackpool.

Once we were in the ground, it was clear that there could be problems ahead as thick frost and ice lay on the pitch under the shade of the Main Stand, and this despite the weak sun which had melted the ice elsewhere on the pitch. And, as the game began and the sun started to set behind the Main Stand, with temperatures dropping like a stone, it quickly became clear that this was a game which might not be played to a conclusion. Proceedings might have been OK on parts of the pitch but were definitely not OK close to the Main Stand, with players slipping and sliding all over the place. If it had not been so serious, it might have been funny to watch, and although many of us had been used to seeing League games being played on snow-covered surfaces in those days, this was something completely different and somewhat sinister. I recall the referee speaking to his linesman under the Main Stand on a couple of occasions in the first half, and when, just before half time and the scores level at 1-1, Palace defender John McCormick went head-over-heels with nobody around him, the referee waved his arms apologetically and the game was over. Nobody protested. It was the only time I have seen a game abandoned at Selhurst Park.

Result CPFC 1 Blackpool 1, match abandoned after 43 minutes due to frozen pitch, attendance 18,900, referee John Yates

Postscript

The game was rescheduled for late January 1969 when Palace lost 2-1, partly due to a bad error by the normally dependable Palace goalie John Jackson. However, that game was to prove to be a watershed, as I hope will become evident shortly.

The craggy Scot, John McCormick, was an ever-present in 1968/69

Game 10 – CPFC v Millwall, 19th March 1969, Division 2

The return fixture against Millwall was, as always, eagerly awaited. I recall the game was re-arranged for some reason, and the delay undoubtedly benefited Palace as - by the time the Millwall game took place - they had strung together six wins and a draw since the Blackpool defeat and were very much in the hunt for promotion.

If the game at The Den had been a 'war of attrition', the return fixture at Selhurst Park on a March evening was pure entertainment and played in front of a raucous crowd of over 32,000. By then, the new Arthur Wait stand was taking shape and I recall standing under the new roof for the first time. Goals went in at both ends, chances were missed and the game ebbed and flowed throughout the ninety minutes. In the second half and with the score 2-2, Palace were awarded a free kick on the edge of the Millwall penalty area and quite central to the goal. Step forward Colin Taylor, a recent acquisition from Walsall and a player with a fearsome left foot. It was probably with some trepidation that the Millwall players lined up to form a wall, the whistle blew and then… Wham… some of the Millwall players must have ducked as the ball exploded past them and crashed into the net with the goalie rooted to the spot. How we cheered. It only remained for John McCormick, surely one of Bert Head's shrewdest acquisitions, to complete the scoring and the Palace quest for promotion was still very much alive.

If ever there was a game where the referee added to the entertainment, this was it. A small, balding, somewhat rotund but extremely fit man with huge sideburns, Roger Kirkpatrick from Leicester, or 'Mr Pickwick' as he was often known, was well known in the 1960s and 1970s for his eccentric refereeing, with his sprints and exaggerated gestures drawing cheers and roars of laughter and approval from the terraces. Sadly, we shall never see the likes of him again at the top level, but his memory lives on to this day, with this 1973 photo showing him in typical pose.

Result CPFC 4 Millwall 2, attendance 32,500, referee Roger Kirkpatrick.

(Photo by Robert Stiggins and printed under licence)

Game 11 – CPFC v Middlesbrough, 4th April 1969, Division 2

The Palace push for promotion continued, and a Roger Hoy goal at South London promotion rivals Charlton ensured a precious point in a 1-1 draw. And, despite being pegged back – 1-1 again - by a last-gasp and controversial Oxford equaliser at Selhurst Park which led to trouble outside after the game, Palace were still in pole-position to accompany the champions elect – Derby County – into Division 1 when they lined up against Middlesbrough on Good Friday 1969.

The Boro were, like Charlton, in the running for promotion and a large crowd was expected, despite an unusually early kick-off time for a bank holiday. As it was Good Friday, I suspect some prayers were said beforehand that absences from church would go unnoticed and by the time the teams emerged on to the pitch, a crowd of over 43,000 had assembled in the warm early Spring sunshine, comfortably a record crowd then for a League game at Selhurst Park. Sadly, the crowd did not include my Boro-supporting dad for some reason.

So what entertainment did we see? Well, I can say with some certainty that there was precisely none to speak of. A fine cross from the Boro left was clawed away by John Jackson from the head of an advancing Boro forward but, since this was actually an ambitious and misplaced back-pass from Palace stalwart David Payne in days when back-passes could be handled by goalkeepers, I do not think this could be classed as part of any 'entertainment'; and since it was not goal-bound anyway, I can say with some certainty that this was a game without a single shot on target. The 'wow' factor? Well, this had to be the most boring game I have ever seen at Selhurst Park, comfortably beating FA Cup ties against Orient and Burnley into 2nd and 3rd places, and I know others have agreed with me about this over the years. No wonder a national newspaper gave it a '1-star' rating the following day, the lowest rating available. My dad must have been chortling at home and perhaps it would have been better if the rest of us had stayed at home or been in church to say our prayers.

A word about the referee – Dr Dennis Brady was a medical practitioner from Gloucester, and he was certainly the only doctor I have ever seen in charge of a League match. The game was one of his last on the League list and, fortunately, he did not have any 'medical emergencies' to deal with during the ninety minutes.

Result CPFC 0 Middlesbrough 0, attendance 43,400, referee Dennis Brady

The first team fixtures and results, as they appeared before the Middlesbrough game in April 1969

FIRST TEAM FIXTURES & RESULTS

FOOTBALL LEAGUE DIVISION 2

Aug.	10—Cardiff City	A	4—0
,,	14—**Huddersfield Town**	H	2—1
,,	17—**Birmingham City**	H	3—2
,,	20—Middlesbrough	A	0—4
,,	24—Bury	A	1—2
,,	28—**Norwich**	H	2—0
,,	31—**Charlton Athletic**	H	3—3
Sept.	7—**Carlisle**	H	5—0
,,	13—Fulham	A	0—1
,,	21—**Preston**	H	1—2
,,	28—Portsmouth	A	3—3
Oct.	5—**Sheffield United**	H	1—1
,,	9—Norwich	A	1—0
,,	12—Aston Villa	A	1—1
,,	19—**Bristol City**	H	2—1
,,	26—Blackpool	A	0—3
Nov.	2—**Bolton Wanderers**	H	2—1
,,	9—Oxford	A	2—0
,,	16—**Blackburn**	H	1—0
,,	23—Millwall	A	2—0
,,	30—**Derby**	H	1—2
Dec.	7—Hull	A	0—2
,,	14—**Aston Villa**	H	4—2
,,	26—Sheffield United	A	1—1
Jan.	11—Bolton Wanderers	A	2—2
,,	25—**Blackpool**	H	1—2
Feb.	22—**Hull**	H	2—0
,,	25—Bristol City	A	1—1
Mar.	1—**Cardiff City**	H	3—1
,,	5—Derby	A	1—0
,,	8—Birmingham	A	1—0
,,	15—**Bury**	H	1—0
,,	19—**Millwall**	H	4—2
,,	22—Charlton A.	A	1—1
,,	26—**Oxford**	H	1—1
,,	29—Carlisle	A	2—1
Apr.	4—**Middlesbrough** 11 a.m.	H	......
,,	5—**Portsmouth**	H	......
,,	8—Huddersfield	A	......
,,	12—Preston North End	A	......
,,	19—**Fulham**	H	......
,,	28—Blackburn	A	......

FOOTBALL LEAGUE CUP

Sept.	4—(2) **Preston**	H	3—1
,,	24—(3) Orient	A	1—0
Oct.	16—(4) **Leeds**	H	2—1
,,	30—(5) Burnley	A	0—2

F.A. CHALLENGE CUP

Jan.	4—(3) Charlton A.	A	0—0
,,	8—(3) Charlton A.	H	0—2

Game 12 – CPFC v Fulham, 19th April 1969, Division 2

The Palace charge towards promotion continued and, by the time Fulham came to Selhurst Park on the last Saturday of the season, the team knew what they had to do - win – to guarantee promotion to Division 1 for the first time.

The Fulham team that arrived at Selhurst Park were but a shadow of the side of the early 1960s and were already doomed to playing in Division 3 the following season, their second successive relegation. The side included Johnny Byrne, still a neighbour of mine, but now clearly nearing the end of his time in League football following his transfer from the Palace at the back end of the previous season. I was sorry to see a player that I regarded as a friend in these difficult circumstances, but there could be no room for sentiment as I made my way on to the terraces with 36,000 others for what promised to be a 'victory parade' for the home team. So what could possibly go wrong?

Well, Fulham for a start, as the doomed away side took the game to Palace in the first half and went in at half time with a deserved 2-0 lead, much to the anguish of most of the fans in the ground. Visions of Oldham in 1964 came to mind, and trannies must have been switched on at half time to see how Charlton were getting on, the South London neighbours being the only realistic rivals to Palace's charge to promotion with champions Derby County.

Whatever manager Bert Head said to the team at the interval or whatever was put in the half time cup of tea, it clearly worked as Steve Kember scored an early goal to put the home side back in the game. It was perhaps fitting that Palace favourite Mark Lazarus should score the equaliser and then, to roars of encouragement from the terraces, immediately set off on his customary lap of honour around the pitch. It only remained for another Palace favourite, Cliff Jackson, to score what was to be the winning goal, and the Palace dream had been realised. They would be playing in Division 1 the next season for the very first time and the celebrations could well and truly begin.

Of course, we all streamed on to the pitch at the end of the game and waited for the Palace players to appear in the Directors' box to take a bow. As in 1964, It took a while for them to appear and then, to the delight of all, they started to strip off their Palace shirts and throw them into the crowd below. With encouragement from the fans, it seemed some would go further, but perhaps a word from the Directors persuaded them otherwise and decency and commonsense prevailed. It was a long while before the players left the box and the crowd dispersed, but what fun and entertainment we were treated to that afternoon.

Result CPFC 3 Fulham 2, attendance 36,100, referee Harry New

Postscript

Palace may have secured promotion with this well-publicised home win on the last Saturday of the season, however, a lesser-known fact is that they could have lost the game against Fulham and still secured promotion, since they still had one game to play, a re-arranged game at Blackburn after the original game was abandoned because of rain and mud; and, bizarrely, the game was played a full nine days after the Fulham match. Did we really care? It seems not since the game was watched by just 4,800 fans, easily the lowest attendance to see Palace play that season. Maybe we were all still celebrating at home, but those fans who made the long trip north were rewarded with a 2-1 win to complete a sequence of sixteen games without defeat which had started after the re-arranged game against Blackpool in January 1969.

The appointment of Bert Head in April 1966 and the Board's decision to stick with him after two fairly lean seasons had paid dividends in the end, and Bert was undoubtedly helped in no small regard by having a small and relatively stable squad of players during the promotion season. It remained to be seen whether this squad could cope with the pressures of top-flight football, but for the moment, manager, players and fans could all celebrate a momentous time in Palace history.

One of my all-time favourites, goalie John Jackson, who was another ever-present during Palace's promotion season in 1968/9

Game 13 – CPFC v Asante Kotoko, 30th July 1969, Friendly

It was not just league and cup games that I attended in those early days of supporting the Palace and, on the third anniversary of England's most famous victory on the football field and ten days before the start of the 1969/70 season, my friends and I ventured to Selhurst Park to see Palace play the champions of Ghana, Asante Kotoko, in an evening friendly match. Friendlies were much more widespread in those days, and they included home games against a Caribbean FA XI in 1959, where my friend Martin saw the away side playing without boots or other footwear and Palace won 11-1, and a 6-3 win against an International XI in 1967 for George Petchey's Testimonial, which I attended.

Having arrived at Selhurst Park just before kick-off on a warm summer's evening, my friends and I made our way towards the open terraces of the Holmesdale Road end to find, to our amazement, a huge mass of fans already in place who were clearly supporting the champions of Ghana. We thought about heading to one of the other terraces, but the game was about to start and we decided to stay put.

I remember little about the game other than that it proved to be a most enjoyable experience. If we were concerned that we were in the middle of a crowd of fans supporting the away side, we should not have been and, as the game progressed, we even ended up participating in the singing and dancing on the terraces, with not a swear word or threat of violence to be heard or seen. It quickly became obvious that Palace would win, and when Asante Kotoko scored a late but deserved goal to bring the score to a respectable 1-3, we all joined in the cheering and roars of approval. It was not just on the pitch that there were handshakes and hugs at the end, and we headed homewards thoroughly satisfied with the evening's entertainment. However, it was now time to look forward to greater things as Palace's first season in the top-flight beckoned.

Result CPFC 3 Asante Kotoko 1, attendance c 5000.

Postscript

I have not been able to locate a programme for the game against Asante Kotoko, but this section of the match programme against the Caribbean FA XI in October 1959, mentioned above, may be of interest. Note the price! It comes c/o Martin Everett.

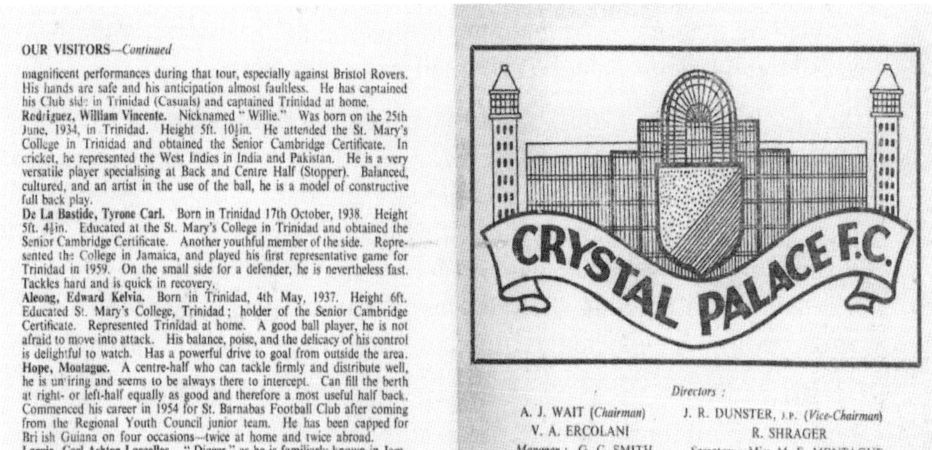

OUR VISITORS—*Continued*

magnificent performances during that tour, especially against Bristol Rovers. His hands are safe and his anticipation almost faultless. He has captained his Club side in Trinidad (Casuals) and captained Trinidad at home.

Rodriguez, William Vincente. Nicknamed "Willie." Was born on the 25th June, 1934, in Trinidad. Height 5ft. 10½in. He attended the St. Mary's College in Trinidad and obtained the Senior Cambridge Certificate. In cricket, he represented the West Indies in India and Pakistan. He is a very versatile player specialising at Back and Centre Half (Stopper). Balanced, cultured, and an artist in the use of the ball, he is a model of constructive full back play.

De La Bastide, Tyrone Carl. Born in Trinidad 17th October, 1938. Height 5ft. 4½in. Educated at the St. Mary's College in Trinidad and obtained the Senior Cambridge Certificate. Another youthful member of the side. Represented the College in Jamaica, and played his first representative game for Trinidad in 1959. On the small side for a defender, he is nevertheless fast. Tackles hard and is quick in recovery.

Aleong, Edward Kelvin. Born in Trinidad, 4th May, 1937. Height 6ft. Educated St. Mary's College, Trinidad; holder of the Senior Cambridge Certificate. Represented Trinidad at home. A good ball player, he is not afraid to move into attack. His balance, poise, and the delicacy of his control is delightful to watch. Has a powerful drive to goal from outside the area.

Hope, Montague. A centre-half who can tackle firmly and distribute well, he is untiring and seems to be always there to intercept. Can fill the berth at right- or left-half equally as good and therefore a most useful half back. Commenced his career in 1954 for St. Barnabas Football Club after coming from the Regional Youth Council junior team. He has been capped for British Guiana on four occasions—twice at home and twice abroad.

Largie, Carl Ashton Lascelles. "Digger," as he is familiarly known in Jamaica, is 31 years old. He was educated at St. George's College in Kingston, Jamaica, and represented Jamaica in Haiti in 1950 and in Trinidad in 1958 and 1959. He is a half back who can play at right half, left half, or centre half. He is a very experienced player and is expected to be very useful on a tour of this kind.

Leggard, Leonard. Born in Trinidad, 19th January, 1930. His height is 5ft. 4½in. Educated in Trinidad at the Belmont Primary School. Represented Trinidad at home in 1959. Had a very good season for his local Club which culminated in his selection for his first tour away from home. Is full of confidence and makes good use of the open spaces. His hobbies are reading, movies and swimming.

Haynes, Reginald F. Born 22nd November, 1931. Represented Barbados against British Guiana in 1953 and 1954; against South Trinidad in 1957 and 1958. Took part in the recent Quadrangular Tournament in order to select the team for this Tour. He displayed good ball control and is more than useful as a right side player. He is expected to do well in the Tour.

Corneal, Alvin Alasley. Born in Trinidad 13th October, 1937. Height 5ft. 8½in. A very versatile forward particularly on the left side. Represented Trinidad at home in 1959. His maiden tour abroad. A natural ball player. Is fast and has great power in his left foot. Also a very useful all-round cricketer. Swimming, dancing and table tennis are his hobbies.

Gray, Ronald James. Born in England on the 13th October, 1939. One of the youngest members of the team, is now resident in Trinidad. Educated at Trinity Academy School, Pointe-A-Pierre, Trinidad. Cambridge Overseas School Certificate. Height 5ft. 9½in. A clever player who oft-times splits a defence. Very dangerous in the area with his head and feet.

Parker, Alan Owen. Born 21st September, 1932. Represented Jamaica in 1953 against the English Football Association. Played for Jamaica against Argentine, Zurich and Milwaukee; also visited Haiti. His first position is outside left, but due to the fact that he is able to use both his feet to advantage he can also fill the role of centre-forward.

Printed by The Andress Printing Co., Ltd., Waddon New Road, Croydon, Surrey

CRYSTAL PALACE F.C.

Directors:

A. J. WAIT (*Chairman*) J. R. DUNSTER, J.P. (*Vice-Chairman*)
V. A. ERCOLANI R. SHRAGER

Manager: G. C. SMITH *Secretary:* Miss M. E. MONTAGUE
Trainer: J. BLACKMAN *Asst. Trainer:* T. BROLLY
Medical Officer: P. SOMMERVILLE, M.B., Ch.B.

WEDNESDAY, 14th OCTOBER, 1959

FLOODLIGHT FRIENDLY

CRYSTAL PALACE

v.

CARIBBEAN F.A. XI

Kick-off 7.30 p.m.

OFFICIAL PROGRAMME – Threepence

Game 14 – CPFC v Manchester United, 9th August 1969, Football League Division 1

I have always looked forward to seeing the League fixtures when they are first published, and it must have been of particular interest to me in June 1969 when the fixtures for the 1969/70 season appeared in the daily newspapers. And there it was in black-and-white, Palace would be playing at home to Manchester United in the first game of their first season in Division 1, and of course I had to be there.

At the start of the 1969/70 season, United were in the throes of a big change at the top, with the legendary Matt Busby retiring a couple of months earlier and his place as manager taken by Wilf McGuinness. In the previous season, they had finished just 11th in Division 1, a disappointing season by their exacting standards. However, the side still contained legends such as Best, Charlton and Law and a record attendance was expected at Selhurst Park to see whether the 'upstarts' of South London could vanquish the 'giants' from Manchester.

I cannot recall for certain, but I am sure I would have been standing on the terraces in the Arthur Wait Stand by about 1pm, fully two hours before kick-off. It was a boiling hot August day and, despite the shade under the new roof, I must have been hoping that I would survive the next four hours without keeling over and needing to be tended by the St John Ambulance staff in front of the fans near the touchline, as was the custom in those days.

At last the teams emerged from the tunnel and a fresh and momentous chapter in Palace history could begin. Of course the Match of the Day cameras were there on this historic occasion - with commentary from Barry Davies – and so, much to my delight, I have been able to watch the highlights again over fifty years later on YouTube.

As with Nottingham Forest in 1965, Palace quickly made it clear that they were not there with the likes of Best and Charlton to make up the numbers, and in the twelfth minute, they opened the scoring, their first ever goal in Division 1. It was perhaps a pity that there was some dispute about who scored the goal, was it Mel Blyth with a looping header from a corner or did Roger Hind get a touch before the ball crossed the line? The official statistics gave the goal to Mel, but did we really care? A rhetorical question as we sang and danced on the packed terraces.

Manchester United may have had a mediocre season, but they quickly responded to this early setback and it was perhaps inevitable that the great Bobby Charlton should draw them level. No problem for the 'upstarts' though as a fine end-to-end move was finished off by Palace favourite Gerry Queen, no doubt about that one and the Palace went in at half time 2-1 up.

If the first half had been a shock for the great United side, they quickly gathered themselves together and the second half was filled with tension on the terraces as the Palace team tried to hang on to what they had fought for in the first half. Ultimately, they did not quite succeed, as a rare mistake from John Jackson let in Willie Morgan for the equaliser and the game ended 2-2.

Were we disappointed at the loss of a point? No, definitely not. Would it be a hard season? Yes, quite probably, but for a while, we could bask in the glory of gaining our first point in the top-flight and sending the great United back to Manchester with something to think about.

Result CPFC 2 Manchester United 2, attendance 48,600 (ground record), referee Harry New

Postscript

Palace's first win in the top-flight was not long coming, four days to be precise as goals from Colin Taylor and Cliff Jackson gave them a 2-0 win over Sunderland in another home game which I saw. However, that was about as good as it got and there were only two further wins in the

League before the team lined up for the return fixture against Manchester United in February 1970.

The 'Rate the Ref' website, to which I contribute, has regular discussions about how often top-flight referees such as Michael Oliver and Anthony Taylor visit individual Premier League grounds during a season. Fully professional referees were first seen when the Premier League was set up in the 1990s and, with a current squad of about twenty 'SG1' referees, it is inevitable that some top-flight referees visit individual grounds several times in a season. In days of old, refereeing appointments were much more widely spread and it is perhaps strange, even unique, that Harry New refereed two consecutive home Palace league games, v Fulham and v Manchester United, albeit in different divisions and with a gap of almost four months. But Harry, from Portsmouth and later Bristol, was a dependable and fair-minded referee and he was a regular and welcome visitor to Selhurst Park during his fifteen years on the League list.

Game 15 - Manchester United v CPFC, 14th Feb 1970, Division 1

In all my first twenty years of life, I never once visited Manchester. However, in February 1970, with the Palace in Division 1 for the first time, the opportunity was there to attend the return game from August 1969 at Old Trafford. My friend Philip and I could have gone on the club coach from South Norwood, but Philip was still having nightmares from his two-night trip to Carlisle in 1966 and we were both earning money by then, and so it was to Euston that we headed for the train north to Manchester.

I am not sure whether it was raining when we arrived in Manchester, but I do recall having a ghastly fish-and-chip lunch in the centre of the city, no fast-food outlets around in those days, before we headed to Old Trafford ready for a 3pm kick off.

Once inside the ground, we found ourselves standing high up in one of the stands surrounded by a mass of United fans, no segregation of fans in those days, and - perhaps quite wisely – we kept quiet as the teams emerged separately from the tunnel.

By this time in the season, Palace were in trouble, with their last win as long ago as November 1969 and, as expected, the first half was embarrassingly one-sided as United first scored - a strike by Brian Kidd from the edge of the penalty area after George Best had turned the Palace defence inside-out – and then did everything but score again, with John Jackson performing heroics in the Palace goal. How the score remained 1-0 was anybody's guess, but that is what it was at half time, and for the first time, Philip and I could see some rays of hope.

The second half continued in the same pattern as the first, but we could sense some growing unease in the United fans around us as chance after chance was squandered. And then it happened, with big-signing but error-prone Ian Ure back-heading the ball woefully in midfield and Palace striker Cliff Jackson latching on to the ball and heading towards the goal beneath us and past the United goalie Alex Stepney before being brought down by the despairing keeper. Penalty! We could have roared our approval but thought better of it. But now there was a problem as it became clear that the vital kick would be taken by Palace captain John Sewell, also known as 'The Duke' for his immaculate dress sense and, with the greatest respect, John was a not a player known for his goal-scoring prowess, even from the penalty spot. The crowd hushed as John stepped forward and then sliced the ball with the outside of his boot towards Stepney who had a comfortable save to make to his left. Except that, inexplicably, Alex only parried the ball and it went back out towards John who somehow managed to squeeze the ball under the advancing keeper and over the line into the goal, with the United players nowhere to be seen. 1–1, game on! Were Philip and I happy? You bet. Did we show our delight? Hmm, probably not.

1-1 was how it stayed for the remainder of the game, and Palace had secured another precious point out of United in their fight to stay in Division 1. The home fans were clearly unhappy at the end, but for Philip and I, our journey back south must have been a happy one.

Result Manchester United 1 CPFC 1, attendance 55,300, referee John Thacker

Postscript

The TV cameras were at the Old Trafford game and, as in August 1969, I have been able to relive the highlights over fifty years later. Palace's fight for survival continued to the last day of the season and beyond, and a vital win at home to Manchester City in their last game of the season meant that Sheffield Wednesday had to beat Man City in their last game to send Palace down to Division 2 in their place. Incredibly, this game was to be played a full two weeks after Palace had beaten Man City, and I imagine there were a fair few radios on in South London as the result filtered through some time after 10pm on a midweek evening. And then we heard it - 'Sheffield Wednesday 1 Man City 2' - and Palace were safe for another season, with Wednesday heading down to Division 2. The sighs of relief were not just mine!

Game 16 – CPFC v Blackpool, 2nd September 1970, Division 1

I have always enjoyed attending evening games at Selhurst Park. On occasions in the 1970s, I came straight from work in central London and, as an ever-helpful Palace fan, I always made it my business to guide away fans at Victoria station to the 'Crystal Palace' train before boarding the train …. to Selhurst and the short walk to the ground ("Father, forgive me for I have sinned", as most Palace fans will be able to confirm). Once inside the ground, usually not before 7pm, I would take my place amidst the mass of fans in the Arthur Wait stand and prepare for the action ahead. One notable evening came in January 1970 when a Gerry Queen header enabled Palace to beat mighty Tottenham 1-0 in a 4th round FA Cup replay, and the roars from the 40,000+ Palace fans as the goal went in could probably be heard in Croydon. And a couple of months later, World Cup star Geoff Hurst was one of six players 'booked' by Rolls-Royce owning referee, Ricky Nicholson, in a turgid London derby against West Ham United, and that in days when six cautions in a game were virtually unheard of.

Mention of Palace favourite Gerry Queen brings me to Game 16 and an evening game in September 1970 against Blackpool. If ever there was an early season four-pointer (two points for a win), this was it, with both teams already in trouble towards the bottom of Division 1. Small wonder that there was a crowd of over 26,000 at the game.

The first twenty minutes of the game were largely forgettable. But then, much to our amazement, THWACK, as a fist landed on the jaw of a Blackpool player in midfield and, unsurprisingly, he went down poleaxed. It was immediately evident that Gerry Queen was the culprit and, even in days when a more tolerant attitude was taken towards misconduct on the field, this could not be allowed to go unpunished and a rueful-looking Gerry started to head off towards the tunnel. But hang on a moment as it quickly became clear that the referee, William 'Bill' Castle from the West Midlands, had missed the incident, or at least who had caused it. Surely though one of his linesmen had seen it. But no, they had clearly not seen it either and, with no fourth official or VAR around in those days, it started to dawn on the players and fans that no further action was going to be taken. OK, Mr Castle might have correctly guessed who the culprit was, but guessing has never been part of a referee's remit and, despite the protestations and finger-pointing from the aggrieved Blackpool players, Gerry resumed his place in the Palace attack.

Did we win? Yes, we did and who should score the winning goal with a header ten minutes from time? Yes, it had to be … Gerry Queen!

I have often been amused by some of the headlines in the tabloid press, for example '109 bus found on the moon', with a 'photo' to prove it. One headline that I will not forget in a hurry came the day after the Blackpool game and read 'Queen in brawl at the Palace'. Full marks to the person who thought that one up and cue the reference at the start of the book to our late Queen Elizabeth.

Result CPFC 1 Blackpool 0, attendance 26,300, referee Bill Castle

Postscript

Three wins on the bounce steered Palace up the table, but as in 1969/70, life was always going to be difficult for them in Division 1, and a place outside the relegation area was always going to be something of an achievement. In the end, they survived with three places and eight points to spare and who should be one of the teams who went down at the end of the season? Why Blackpool of course. I must admit I felt sorry for them.

Game 17 – CPFC v Leeds United, 7th November 1970, Division 1

Despite already spilling the beans on the season outcome for the Palace, I want to stay in 1970/71 for one more League game, and that was a Saturday afternoon game against Leeds United. This was another key game but, unlike Blackpool two months earlier, mighty Leeds were already challenging for top spot in the League, and for the Palace fans, little was expected of their team from the game.

Play was predictably one-sided, and it came as a bit of a surprise that Leeds did not score until the second half when Lorimer latched on to a long through ball to head his team in front. There could easily have been more goals, but as the clock ticked down to ninety minutes, the score was still 1-0 and Palace began to mount some attacks with increased urgency, but to no avail (or so it seemed) as the great Jack Charlton and his fellow defenders easily fended off their efforts. And then the ball came out to John Sewell on the edge of the Leeds penalty area and he returned the ball into the area as a hopeful lob. However, the ball was far too close to the Leeds goalie, Welsh international Gary Sprake, who prepared to make a comfortable save above his head. And then, inexplicably, the error-prone Gary dropped the ball over his head and into the goal. 1-1, cue pandemonium! Home fans roared in delight and derision, Gary held his head in his hands and, if looks could kill, Jack Charlton would have been up before the judge at the Old Bailey the next morning. And all in front of the TV cameras. 1-1 was how it stayed, and Palace had secured a precious point in their battle for survival and mighty Leeds had thrown away a point in their quest for the title. Were we happy? You bet we were!

One-sided, error-prone, inexplicable, John Sewell scoring, 1-1 result, now where had I seen this before?

Result CPFC 1 Leeds Utd 1, attendance 38,000, referee Ken Wynn

Postscript

Leeds continued their drive towards the title, but had to settle for runners-up spot after title-winners Arsenal beat North London rivals Tottenham 1-0 in the final game of the season. And the gap between the two teams? One point (65/64) so, indirectly, it could be said that Palace favourite John Sewell had a say in the destination of the League title that season.

Immaculate on the field as well as off, John Sewell played 258 games for the Palace between 1963 and 1971.

Game 18 – Arsenal v CPFC, 9th November 1970, League Cup 3rd round replay

Mention of Arsenal leads me to a League Cup replay against The Gunners just two days after the Leeds match. In those days, League Cup replays were the norm and, having been treated to a rip-roaring tie at Selhurst Park, despite a 0-0 scoreline, it was to Highbury that I headed on a Monday night, hopeful but not very optimistic that we could get a result out of high-flying Arsenal.

The early signs were good as Gerry Queen opened the scoring for the Palace but, as the game progressed through the second half, the pressure on the Palace goal increased and it seemed only a matter of time before Arsenal scored. But then… flashpoint…. Arsenal goalie Bob Wilson had the ball in his hands and Alan Birchenall stood in front of him. Nothing unusual or illegal in that, except that the normally calm and dependable Bob then had a rush of blood to his head and - still holding the ball - planted it firmly into Alan's face who went down in a heap on the ground. If the incident had not taken place immediately beneath me, I would probably not have believed my eyes. But what next? Well, top referee Norman Burtenshaw certainly knew what he was going to do and that was to grab the ball theatrically from Bob and place it firmly on the penalty spot, no whistle or words, no questions asked and no dissent seen as the crestfallen Bob Wilson and his colleagues realised the magnitude of what he had done. It only remained for ace penalty taker Bobby Tambling to deliver the *coup de gras* from the spot and Palace were through 2-0 and a 4th round tie at Old Trafford.

Result Arsenal 0 CPFC 2, attendance 45,000, referee Norman Burtenshaw

Postscript

I actually saw three Palace v Arsenal games in less than three weeks, a League game at Highbury five days after the League Cup replay ending 1-1 on what was surely one of the wettest days I have ever experienced watching my favourite team. The fact that the Palace did not lose any of the three games speaks volumes for their resolve, Arsenal going on to achieve a (then) rare double of League and FA Cup at the end of the season. And I could say I was present when they went out of the one competition which they failed to win.

Game 19 – Aldershot v CPFC, 27th December 1975, Division 3

You may have noticed that I have fast-forwarded again, this time by five years. A lot happened in the interim, Palace were relegated, not once but twice and, by the start of the 1975/6 season, they were back in Division 3. By then, the flamboyant Malcolm Allison was in charge at Selhurst Park and, having overseen the second of the relegations in 1973/4, he almost guaranteed promotion the following season. The signs were good in 1974/5, but ultimately the Palace fell short by two places and four points. However, the club stuck with Malcolm and thus, at the start of the 1975/6 season, they faced the challenges of Bury, Grimsby and Halifax rather than the hoped-for Liverpool, Arsenal and Manchester United.

At this time, I was very active in refereeing and most Saturday afternoons and some midweek evenings were spent at grounds such as Carshalton, Sutton, Horsham and Bromley rather than on the terraces of Selhurst Park.

Two days after Christmas 1975 was a day of celebration for me and, without a game to referee, what better way to spend it than watching the Palace with friends at their post-Christmas game at Aldershot. By then, Palace were going great guns, with only two defeats to their name, and Malcolm's predictions of promotion seemed a realistic proposition. Sadly, one of the defeats had come the week before Christmas at arch-rivals Millwall but, in the greater scheme of things, this seemed to be just a blip, with struggling Aldershot hardly likely to present a further barrier in the quest for promotion. It promised to be a good day.

The afternoon started badly with delays on the roads, and it was fifteen minutes from kick off before we finally arrived in the Army town, hurriedly parked the car in one of the many side roads near the ground and dashed to the turnstiles, only to find a queue waiting to get in. Once inside, it became clear that we would have to struggle through the packed terraces to the far end where a mass of Palace fans was already gathered, and by the time we took our places with the fans, the game was underway. But hey, we had not missed anything.

And then the unthinkable happened, with Aldershot opening the scoring below us in their first attack of the game. No worries, we still had 85 minutes to play, and the home team were fielding a second-string goalie by the name of Johnson, so all would be well in the end, would it not?

Except that all was definitely not well by the end of the first half, with The Shots still leading, Johnson performing heroics in the Aldershot goal, and Hammond at the other end below us a virtual spectator.

Surely the second half would be better, but no, Johnson continued to play out of his skin and the Palace efforts to score a goal became increasingly desperate. And then with five minutes to go, a corner was only half-cleared to the edge of the penalty area and there was Palace favourite Martin Hinshelwood to volley the ball towards the top corner of the Aldershot goal. It was a goal all the way, except that the said Johnson somehow managed to get across and claw the ball away. It was a save that England legend Gordon Banks would have been proud of, the Aldershot players celebrated whilst the Palace players hung their heads in despair and the Palace fans looked on silently in disbelief.

1-0 was how it stayed, and the Palace had suffered a second defeat on the spin and dented their promotion hopes in the process. We made our way back silently to the car through the by-now darkened streets, but where had we left the car? That was the question. It was definitely not an evening of celebration.

Result Aldershot 1 CPFC 0, attendance 14,000, referee Alex Lees

Postscript

The slide continued, with just one League win up to the end of February, and by the time Palace lined up for the return fixture against Aldershot, it was clear that nothing short of a win would do to keep alive their slim hopes of promotion. However, once again the Aldershot defence proved resolute, although whether Johnson played in goal is not known, and a 0-0 draw effectively ended the hopes for the Palace, with another season in Division 3 to come and Malcolm Allison departing for pastures new. He had certainly been a flamboyant manager at Selhurst Park, and his part in getting the Palace to the semi-finals of the FA Cup in 1975/6, with the famous fedora on his head, could certainly not be ignored. However, it was now time for a new person at the helm and that person was to be Terry Venables.

Game 20 – Wrexham v CPFC, 11th May 1977, Division 3

The appointment of Terry Venables, in his first managerial role, proved to be an inspired one and, nearing the end of the 1976/7 season, Palace were in with a definite shout of promotion after three seasons in Division 3. Three potential barriers stood in their way, Mansfield, Wrexham and Brighton, with one of the four teams in contention missing out on promotion. But would that be the Palace? And to add a further twist to the end-of-season quest, the final fixtures of the season included Palace v Wrexham (twice), Wrexham v Brighton and Wrexham v Mansfield. The stakes could not be higher.

I was at the Palace v Wrexham game at Selhurst Park which Palace won 2-1, thanks in part to a frankly ludicrous penalty award by referee Tony Glasson which Paul Hinshelwood converted. So far, so good, and when Wrexham and Brighton cancelled each other out at the Racecourse Ground, the signs looked even more promising. And it was clear then that the return Wrexham v Palace game would be key to deciding who would be promoted and who would not.

At the time of the return fixture, I was in a travelling job, and one advantage of being on the road so much was that I could plan visits to evening games around my work schedules and, on this occasion, I made sure I was working in Manchester for a few days, with a free afternoon to travel out to North Wales for the evening match.

The scenario could not be simpler, Wrexham, unbeaten at home all season, needed just a draw to secure promotion with Mansfield and Brighton, whilst Palace needed a win and hope that Wrexham would drop points against Mansfield a few days later in the final game of the season. Small wonder that over 18,000 fans made their way from the town centre to the ground on a sunny Spring evening.

Having paid to go in, I found myself in the middle of a mass of home fans near the halfway line. I could have struggled through to the end where the Palace fans were assembled but decided to stay put and keep as quiet as I could about my allegiances. The home fans were happy at the prospect of promotion that evening, and I certainly did not want to disturb their mood, at least not until the final whistle.

There was a further hurdle for the Palace to overcome, the regular goalie, Tony Burns, had picked up an injury and a young keeper by the name of Peter Caswell was making his debut for the team. A baptism of fire if ever there was one.

The first half was promising for the Palace, so promising in fact that they had a 2-0 lead, with goals from Swindlehurst and Perrin, and the home crowd was silent. However, Wrexham were not about to give up their hopes of promotion in a hurry and two goals after half time took them towards the point they needed to pip Palace to promotion. And, as the clock ticked down to ninety minutes, 'Land of my Fathers' started to ring round the ground and the Palace dream looked to be over for another season. Then…

It started in midfield with an innocuous challenge, with the ball spinning off a Wrexham defender towards the corner flag. A corner would be good but, strangely, what the Palace really wanted was a throw-in by the corner flag which long throw expert Kenny Sansom could hurl into the Wrexham goalmouth. My heart was in my mouth as the ball drifted towards the flag, hit it and dribbled out ever so slowly for…… a throw-in. Game on! Kenny's long throw to the near post was as accurate as ever, the ball was headed on across the goal and there was Rachid Harkouk to hook the ball in from close range. Cue bedlam at the far end away to my left and silence all around me.

3-2, but amidst the jubilation of the Palace players and fans, it quickly became clear that another Palace goal would mean Wrexham having to beat Champions-elect Mansfield on the following Saturday rather than draw, and it was the Palace players who quickly lined up for the restart. However, only about a minute of added time remained and the chances of a Palace fourth seemed gone. But then… a slip in the Wrexham defence and there was Jeff Bourne bearing down on the Wrexham goal in a one-on-one with the home goalie. Could he beat the goalie and score? You bet he could, 4-2, pandemonium, with a Palace player booked for booting the ball over the stand and out of the ground and Terry Venables on the pitch celebrating and then beating a hasty retreat as the referee moved towards him. And me? Well, I think I allowed myself a whoop of delight as the shell-shocked Wrexham fans quickly made their way to the exits. 4-2 was how it ended and the Palace players could do no more. It was now all down to the last game of the season, Wrexham v Mansfield, which Wrexham had to win.

You sometimes hear people ask, "where were you when…..?" Well, I know exactly where I was when the Wrexham result came through and that was in the middle of the Channel on a booze cruise from Dover to Calais and back. Of course I had my tranny with me, and was looking for a Wrexham draw or defeat, but attempts to hear the results at 5pm proved futile. However, I had the tranny back on - earpiece in place – for the second reading of the results just before 6pm. The noise on the boat and interference on the tranny meant that I could not hear half the results, but then I heard the magic words, "Wrexham 0 …..crackle crackle….". I could not hear any more but it did not matter. Wrexham had failed to score and the Palace were back in Division 2 after three seasons away. The celebrations could start in earnest, and on a booze cruise as well!

Result Wrexham 2 CPFC 4, attendance 18,500, referee Peter Reeves

Postscript

For the record, Wrexham lost 1-0 to Mansfield, with the goal coming from a breakaway in the last few minutes of the game as the home side tried desperately to score the goal which would have earned them promotion in place of Palace. The following season, Wrexham secured promotion with ease and I was pleased for them after the trauma of the final matches of the 1976/7 season. However, it was now time to look forward with the Palace to life in Division 2.

Game 21 – CPFC v Fulham, 28th October 1978, Division 2

The first season back in Division 2 proved to be a mixed one for the Palace, and a halfway finish was probably as good as could be expected. However, the start of the following season was far more promising and, by the time Fulham came to Selhurst Park in late October 1978, Palace were unbeaten in the League. By then, I was no longer refereeing and lining on the 'contributory' leagues and thus had some Saturday afternoons to watch my favourite team in action, and it was to Selhurst Park that I ventured hoping to see the Palace pick up another two points in their push for promotion.

I remember little about the game, only that Palace were 0-1 down as the clock ticked towards ninety minutes, and any hopes of 'doing-a-Wrexham' were extinguished as the referee blew the final whistle, the players trooped towards the tunnel and the fans started to head home, most of them disappointed.

So where was the 'wow' factor? Well, unbeknown to me and many other fans who were already heading to the likes of Selhurst station, there was drama in the tunnel as someone – probably a linesman – pointed out to the referee that he had only played forty minutes in the second half rather than forty-five. And, to the amazement of the fans who had stayed behind, the players and officials then trooped back out onto the pitch to play the remaining five minutes. Needless to say, Palace failed to score in that time and the 0-1 result stood.

Of course many fans, including myself, were completely unaware of the drama that was unfolding at the ground, and I remained oblivious to it until I read or heard about it later that evening. I might have been annoyed, particularly if the Palace had scored, but they had not and the result had stayed the same. So what went wrong? It was an astonishing tale, but it seemed that the referee's watch had stopped early in the second half and, rather than asking one of his linesman for a replacement, he had looked at the clock on the roof of the Arthur Wait stand and, when the clock ticked round to 4.40pm (ten minutes half time in those days), he had assumed that the forty-five minutes were up and blown the final whistle. However, as any longstanding Palace fan could confirm, the clock in question was notoriously unreliable and the actual time was nearer 4.35pm. Why did the referee not realise that there was still time to go, particularly as, in those 'pre-comms' days and lacking any fourth official, he would have received a 'five-minutes-to-go' signal from his linesmen if he had bothered to look at them? We shall probably never know, but it was a basic and huge error, and it was noted that the referee – Eddie Hughes of Weston-super-Mare – came off the League list at the end of the season after a comparatively short time on it. As the Rate the Ref website has always made clear, one bad error does not make for a bad referee, but this mistake would have been difficult to believe at any level and it clearly could not be brushed under the carpet. A routine game at Selhurst Park had drama and a 'wow' factor in it, but I and thousands of other fans did not actually see it.

Result CPFC 0 Fulham 1, attendance 28,700, referee Eddie Hughes

Postscript

Just recently, I heard that the unfortunate Mr Hughes had returned to local football after coming off the League list and was actively involved in football administration in the Weston-super-Mare area for many years after, and I respect and applaud him for that.

Palace quickly put the Fulham defeat behind them and continued their charge towards promotion back to the big time. And on Friday 11th May 1979, they achieved their aim with a win against Burnley at Selhurst Park. There was certainly a 'wow' factor in that game, as 51,500 crowded into the ground, comfortably a ground record. Alas, I was not among them as the game had been re-arranged following an earlier postponement, and I had already booked myself for another event on this Friday evening which I could not get out of. Strangely, it was a football evening at Crystal Palace, but the main town centre rather than close to Selhurst Park. That was probably as well as the horrendous parking problems extended right up to where our event was being held and beyond. And, possibly for the last time, my tranny served a useful purpose during the evening, with a mighty roar coming from our event as Ian Walsh opened the scoring in the last ten minutes and the celebrations could begin. Palace were back in the big time and as Division 2 champions for the first time as well.

Game 22 - CPFC v Liverpool, 26th April 1980, Division 1

Did I tell you about the time I took thirty people to see the Palace play Liverpool in a top-flight game at Selhurst Park? Difficult to believe now in the Premier League, but I did actually do this in 1980.

The start of the 1979/80 season in Division 1 was promising, so promising in fact that when Ipswich were swept aside in late September, Palace were unbeaten and sitting proudly at the top of Division 1 for the first time, and some were already labelling them the 'team-of-the-century'. That was as good as it got and, by the time Liverpool came to Selhurst Park for the last home game of the season in late April 1980, it was the mighty Mersey-siders who were pressing for the title, with Palace comfortably situated just below halfway. It was a game which, it seemed, everyone wanted to see.

At the time, I was involved in youth football and, a month or so before the game, some parents and I decided that it would be good to celebrate the end of a successful season by going to see a game at Selhurst Park, which some of us already frequented. But which game? We had a choice in April 1980, Brighton, Leeds or Liverpool and, possibly due to the logistics of getting everyone and everything organised, we plumped for the last of these, the game against mighty Liverpool, and I was given the task of organising the trip.

The game was played on a Saturday and the day dawned wet, wet, wet, with a dire forecast for the afternoon. We might have wanted to go under the cover of the Arthur Wait or Main stands, but this was not really an option with thirty of us of all ages, and so it was to the (then) open standing terraces of the Whitehorse Lane end that we headed, macs and brollies to hand.

Entry to the Whitehorse Lane end was by way of cash at the turnstiles as it had been in 1962 and, by the time thirty of us accessed the terraces, I half-expected to see a packed crowd in front of us and was more than a little relieved when it became clear that many fans had opted to try and keep dry elsewhere in the ground. There was nothing for it but to stand for the next two hours in the pouring rain and hope that the Palace did not ship too many goals.

I was pleased when it became clear that the game was to be refereed by John Martin from the wonderfully-named Four Marks near Alton in Hampshire. John was an old Croydon colleague (although not apparently a Crystal Palace fan) and I had been out with him many times on the contributory leagues. He was a nice man, an excellent referee, and always fitter than just about anyone else on the Football League referees list, and this later resulted in him being invited to stay on the League list beyond the (then) normal retirement age of 47/48 and into his fifties.

The game began as expected, with Liverpool mounting wave-upon-wave of attacks towards us at the Whitehorse Lane end. However, the Palace defence stood resolute and half time arrived with no goals on the board. The pattern continued in the second half as Liverpool sought the goal which would likely give them the title, but again the Palace refused to buckle. Then, as the game moved into the ninetieth minute, a Liverpool player went down in a heap following a challenge in the Palace penalty area at the far end and we waited with bated breath to see whether John would award a penalty. To our relief, he did not and the game ended 0-0 a minute or two later. Liverpool were clearly not happy, but the very fit John would have been on the spot to make his decision and I know from experience that the decision would have been taken without fear or favour.

A number of the adults and children were attending their first game at Selhurst Park and, at the end of a rain-soaked afternoon, my mind was taken back to my first game at the ground and to the Whitehorse Lane end, with different opponents but the same result, and I hoped that some of the children would, like me, go on to support the Palace in later life. And with an attendance of 45,600 – certainly the last 45,000+ attendance before major redevelopment work took place at the ground - I can say that I was responsible for thirty of them attending that very wet afternoon in 1980.

Result CPFC 0 Liverpool 0, attendance 45,600, referee John Martin

Postscript

As expected, Liverpool won the title back at Anfield the following week, beating Manchester United into second place by two points.

John Martin is pictured right in later years, with refereeing colleague Bill Cleare from High Wycombe and young Lewis, son of Gayle H from the Rate the Ref website.

Game 23 - CPFC v Portsmouth, 4th May 1987, Division 2

The following season – 1980/81 – was a time of turmoil for the Palace, with Terry Venables leaving after a run of seven straight defeats in Division 1, and being replaced successively by Ernie Walley, Malcolm Allison (again) and Dario Gradi, all in one season. And it came as no surprise that the Palace ended up bottom of the Division by a massive thirteen points. I return to Dario later in the book.

In the following five seasons, Palace adjusted to life in Division 2 under Dario, Steve Kember, Alan Mullery and Steve Coppell. I attended a few games in that time, and dire FA cup ties against Orient and Burnley, and home and away League cup ties against Manchester United, none of which produced a goal for the Palace, come to mind. However, I now move on to 1986/7 and the final home game of the season against Portsmouth.

The scenario could not be clearer, Portsmouth needed just a point to confirm promotion to Division 1 whilst Palace, under Steve Coppell, needed a win and three points, plus a miracle elsewhere, to keep alive their faint hopes of promotion. However, Portsmouth had been on a poor run of form when they came to Selhurst Park and had already blown their one-point guarantee of promotion at Fratton Park, and it was clear that they were far from confident of getting anything out of the Palace that afternoon.

From the start, Portsmouth made their intentions clear, they were there to get the required point, and if it was not entertaining to watch, so be it. And that is what happened for 88 minutes. Then, with two minutes remaining, and the 'Pompey Chimes' beginning to ring round the ground, an innocuous centre came in from the Palace right at the Whitehorse Lane end, and the Pompey defenders stood and watched as the ball went harmlessly across the goal and out towards the goal line for a goal kick. Or so it seemed. However, a Palace player had other ideas and managed to scoop the ball back into the goalmouth where the ever-vigilant Palace legend Ian Wright bundled the ball in from close range. There was an audible and collective gasp as the Palace fans realised that their hopes might still be alive and the Pompey fans that their hopes might well have been dashed, at least for another week. Did the ball go out? All eyes were on the referee and linesman, but they were having none of any Portsmouth protests, and the Palace fans could begin to celebrate. My mind was taken back to Wrexham ten years previously and, if ever there was a 'groundhog-day', this was it.

It might be thought that the drama was over for the day but no, as the game moved into added time, former Palace legend, Vince Hilaire, who was playing for Portsmouth by then, got involved in a scuffle in midfield and was sent off. I was sad that his return to the club he had served with distinction for eight years was ending in this way. However, there could be no room for sentiment, and it only remained for Palace to see out the last few moments of the game before the Pompey fans could depart silent and disappointed and the Palace fans look for results from elsewhere and hope that their promotion hopes might still be alive.

Result CPFC 1 Portsmouth 0, attendance 18,000, referee Rob Hamer

Postscript

Portsmouth secured the point they needed the following week at Fratton Park whilst results did not go the way of Palace, and their defeat at Hull was academic with sixth place being secured. In later years, this would have been sufficient to see them in the play-off semi-finals, but this was the first season the play-offs were held and the Palace were not involved. Another season in Division 2 beckoned.

Game 24 - CPFC v Blackburn, 3rd June 1989, Division 2 Play-off Final, 2nd leg.

Two more seasons passed with Steve Coppell as manager and, towards the end of the second season – 1988/9 - Palace were firmly in the hunt for promotion back to the big-time. In the end, they were pipped at the post by Manchester City who went up with Chelsea, and Palace were left to try and secure the third promotion spot via the play-offs.

By now, the format for the play-offs was more-or-less what it is now, the main difference being that the Final was played over two legs, home and away. After a stuttering start, Swindon were swept aside in the semi-final, with Blackburn providing the opposition in the Final and the second leg at Selhurst Park. I did not attend the away leg at Ewood Park which Palace lost 1-3, but of course I had to be at the second leg which was played in front of 30,000 fans in early June 1989, and with the TV cameras there to record every minute.

There were obvious tensions on the terraces at the start, but Ian Wright soon helped the Palace cause with a goal midway through the first half. However, Palace needed a second goal to take the game to extra time and Blackburn were proving to be stubborn opponents, and it was not until the second half that Dave Madden slotted home a penalty to take the game to the extra half hour. It was a 'soft' award from the normally dependable referee George Courtney, but did we care? Game on! By now, the tension was becoming unbearable on the packed terraces. Would the game go to penalties? Not if Ian Wright had his way, and with just two minutes remaining in extra time, he headed home a cross and the Palace were back in Division 1 after eight seasons away. Small wonder that there were pitch invasions when the goal went in and again at the end.

Result CPFC 3 Blackburn 0, attendance 30,000, referee George Courtney

Postscript

After the celebrations finally ended, I made my way out of the ground, thinking that I would be back the following season to watch the likes of Liverpool and Arsenal. However, the game against Blackburn proved to be my last at Selhurst Park for ten years as my work took me to the Northwest of England in the following September. And by the time I returned to Selhurst Park, it was a very different place to how I left it in June 1989. More on that shortly.

Game 25 - Manchester City v CPFC, 22nd Dec 1990, Division 1

My move north meant that visits to see the Palace had to take a back seat, and I watched their memorable win against Liverpool in the FA Cup semi-final in April 1990, followed by the Final and replay at Wembley, on TV rather than live. I would have liked to have been at Villa Park to see the semi-final, but at least the whole game was shown live on the BBC, the first time that a semi had featured in this way.

The first season back in Division 1 was mixed, but by the following season – 1990/1 - the combination of the deadly duo - Wright and Bright – saw the Palace heading towards the top of the division and, with a free Saturday just before Christmas, I decided to head to Maine Road, then the home of Manchester City, to see the Palace in action.

I recall the game had two 'wow' factors. The first came when there was a comical mix-up in the City defence which led to a defender planting a through ball firmly into his own net as City goalie Tony Coton rushed out towards him to claim it. The Palace players and fans celebrated, but I did not join in since I had purchased a ticket in the Main Stand with the City fans. Then, midway through the second half, Ian Wright picked up the ball in midfield and set off towards the City goal. On and on he went before planting the ball into the corner of the net past the despairing Coton. It was a goal worthy of winning any game and indeed, when it came to the end of the season, it was judged 'goal of the season' on Match of the Day, a very worthy winner from the Palace legend which I was pleased to have seen. The City fans may not have been pleased with the outcome, but I certainly was.

Result Man City 0 CPFC 2, attendance 25,300, referee Kieran Barratt

Postscript

The Palace season continued apace, with a home win against high-flying Liverpool being shown on terrestrial TV just a week after the City game. Ultimately, defeats at Arsenal and Liverpool cost them and meant that they had to settle for third place in Division 1 behind their illustrious opponents. Ordinarily, this would have earned them a place in Europe, but this was the period when English clubs were in the wilderness post-Heysel and games in Europe were but a distant memory and dream. However, the Palace had done well under Steve Coppell, and they also had a Cup to their name, more about that in my next game.

Game 26 - CPFC v Everton, 7th April 1991, Zenith Data Systems Cup Final

Did I tell you about the time I saw the Palace win a Cup at Wembley? No, I am not talking about recent times, rather April 1991, and the Zenith Data Systems Cup which they proudly took back to Selhurst Park. The Full Members Cup, as it was initially known, was set up in 1985/6 to be contested by the teams in Divisions 1 and 2. From the start, little priority was given to the competition, and Palace faltered at the first hurdle in each of the first three seasons. However, a run to the semi-finals in 1989/90 was followed by a similar run in the following season, and on this occasion, Norwich were beaten to set up a Final appearance at Wembley against Everton. And with a 'Cup Final' appearance in prospect, albeit not the FA Cup Final of the previous season, my friends and I decided to go.

The game was to be played on a Sunday afternoon, and it was down the newly- opened M40 extension from Birmingham that my friends and I travelled on the morning of the match. We half-expected to see a load of Everton scarves on the way and, perhaps wisely, we kept our Palace scarves away from public view, but it was actually the Palace scarves that we saw in greater quantity, and it quickly became clear that my friends and I were not the only Palace fans going to the game who had relocated away from South London.

It was my first visit to Wembley since I had won a ticket to see Sunderland play Leeds in the 1973 FA Cup Final, and the atmosphere before the game was similar to that memorable afternoon eighteen years previously. The National Anthem was sung with gusto, the teams were introduced to the dignitaries, and it was then time for action in front of a sizeable crowd of over 50,000.

The first half lacked goals, but it certainly had its moment of controversy as Andy Thorn dumped an Everton attacker on the ground as he went flying down the wing and we waited to see whether the Palace would be reduced to ten men or Thorn would be allowed to continue. Fortunately, referee George Courtney decided on yellow, much to our relief and the annoyance of the Everton fans. This was the same George who had awarded the Palace a 'soft' penalty in the 1989 Division 2 Play-off Final and had refereed Palace's famous victory over Liverpool in the 1990 FA Cup semi-final, and I think it is fair to say that George was something of a lucky charm for the Palace.

It was midway through the second half before we saw a goal and it came courtesy of a header from Palace captain Geoff Thomas that gave his side the lead. However, before we could celebrate, Everton stormed back to equalise. The tension mounted as the game moved on, and two magnificent saves, one at each end, ensured that the scores would remain level until the end of ninety minutes and the start of extra time.

If extra time was to be a cagey affair between two teams frightened of losing, nobody had told the Palace players, and a goal from Ian Wright towards the end of the first period gave Palace a deserved lead again. And this time, there was to be no response from Everton, and goals from Salako and another from Wright in the second period ensured that it would be the Palace, led by Geoff Thomas, who would be climbing the famous stairs at the end to receive the Cup, the first at Wembley in their history. It may only have been the Zenith Data Systems Cup, but hey, were we pleased, and it was certainly a happy bunch of Palace fans who made their way back north later that evening.

Result CPFC 4 Everton 1, attendance 52,500, referee George Courtney

Postscript

The Full Members Cup survived for only one more season and Palace were one of only five winners of the Cup, Chelsea (twice), Nottingham Forest (twice), Blackburn and Reading being the others. The competition may have been long forgotten, but that day in April 1991, when the Palace won a Cup for the first time at Wembley, is remembered by many fans to this day.

Game 27 - CPFC v Nottingham Forest, 27th Nov 1999, Division 1

You may have noticed that I have moved on over eight years to season 1999/2000, and this is because I am fairly certain that I did not see any Palace games in the interim. A lot happened at Selhurst Park in those eight years, Palace were promoted and relegated no less than three times, they played in the new Premier League in three seasons and went straight back down each time and, by 1999/2000, they were in Division 1, but not the Division 1 of former years, rather what was later to become the Championship as a second tier to the Premier League. Confused? I certainly was and it was perhaps little wonder that the club was known as the 'Palace of Varieties', with growing financial issues and frequent managerial changes contributing to the problems at Selhurst Park.

One link between 1991 and 1999 was manager Steve Coppell who returned to the club in January 1999, and it was Steve who was in charge as I made my way back to Selhurst Park for my first visit there in over ten years. As I walked up from Selhurst station to meet my friends at the ground, I was immediately struck by the new stand roof appearing out of the gloom of a November afternoon at the Holmesdale Road end. However, it was to the old Main Stand that I made my way for the game against Nottingham Forest. It was not of course the first time that I had been in the Main Stand and, although some improvements had been made since I had last been there, not least safety aspects following the Bradford City fire tragedy, I was immediately struck by how old fashioned it all looked, in particular the shower unit located in the Gents toilet, and I wondered whether any Palace fans had ever tried to use it before or after a match. Probably not! Further changes included the players entering and exiting the pitch from the Holmesdale Road end rather than the Main Stand by the halfway line, and players and officials entering the pitch together at the start of the game.

Palace were struggling a bit in the second tier before the game and so were Forest who had appointed David Platt as manager after being relegated from the Premier League at the end of the previous season, and three points were seen as a key outcome for both sides. It was the Palace who took the game to the visitors and the Swede, Mathias 'Matt' Svensson, who gave the home team the lead shortly after half time. Former Palace Junior, Leon McKenzie, extended the lead and cries of 'sacked in the morning' could then be heard aimed at David Platt in the Forest dugout. 2-0 was the final score and my first visit back to Selhurst Park had ended with a deserved victory.

Result CPFC 2 Nottingham Forest 0, attendance 15,900, referee Paul Rejer.

Game 28 - Crewe Alexandra v CPFC, 16th Dec 2000, Division 1

Both Palace and Forest survived to fight another season in Division 1. However, by the start of the following season, Alan Smith had taken up the reins again as Palace manager, and thoughts must have turned to his previous stint at the club which included winning the Division 1 title in May 1994.

In August 2000, I moved to the railway town of Crewe to be with my now wife Marta and thoughts soon turned to attending some games at my local club, Crewe Alexandra. At the time, the 'Alex' were also in Division 1, under their popular manager Dario Grady, yes, the same Dario who had managed the Palace almost twenty years previously. Thus, just before Christmas 2000, I made my way to Gresty Road, a half-hour walk from home, for the Crewe Alex v Crystal Palace fixture. This game presented an obvious problem, should I go with the Palace fans in the Away Stand or in the Main Stand with the home fans, some of whom I already knew from my short time in the town? I plumped for the comparative security and comfort of the Main Stand, which had been opened just a year or so previously and was positively luxurious compared with its counterpart at Selhurst Park. As at Old Trafford and Maine Road, I clearly needed to watch what I said and did during the game.

The first half was all Alex and the Palace problems grew on the half-hour when the combative Neil 'Razor' Ruddock said something unpleasant to the referee, the comparatively inexperienced Mike Dean, and received a straight red card for what is described in the trade as 'foul and abusive language'. Five minutes later, a Crewe player went down in the penalty area and Mike pointed dramatically to the spot. Inward groans from me and roars of approval from the fans around me. I held my breath but need not have worried as the ball came back off the bar and was cleared to safety. However, the relief was short-lived as the Alex took a deserved lead just before the interval, and the cups of tea and Bovril could then be enjoyed by the home fans in the modern hall underneath the stand.

If the first half had been all Alex, the second half was much more about the Palace as they woke up to the possibility of losing for the first time in nine League games. However, Crewe were not about to lie down and die and I could see Alan Smith getting more and more agitated on the touchline as the half progressed. Then, with just five minutes remaining, Dougie Freedman equalised and that was how the game ended, 1-1. Everybody, it seemed, was happy as they made their way out of the ground and back to the station or home.

Result Crewe Alexandra 1 CPFC 1, attendance 5,800, referee Michael Dean

Postscript

Alan Smith continued as manager at Selhurst Park but left at the end of April 2001 after a poor run of results which saw the Palace in imminent danger of relegation and needing to win their final two games of the season to avoid the drop. Steve Kember took over as caretaker manager for these final two matches and, miracle-upon-miracle, Palace first beat Portsmouth away 4-2, and then won 1-0 at Stockport in their must-win final game of the season, with the very late and controversial winner coming from none other than Dougie Freedman. What an asset he was. Needless to say, despite the proximity of Stockport to my home town, I was not there to see them stay up amidst much celebration at the end.

I do not recall attending any further games at Gresty Road that season, but I was to become a regular attender there in later years and was to see two further Crewe v Palace fixtures, including one which forms my story for Game 30.

Referee Mike Dean may have been comparatively inexperienced in 2000, but we were to see a lot more of him in subsequent years, and he was always regarded as one of the best referees in the country until his retirement in May 2022 after twenty-five years as a top-flight official.

Game 29 - CPFC v Stoke City, 14th February 2004, Division 1

Another season and another visit to Selhurst Park to report on. Since my visit in 1999, the managerial merry-go-round had continued, and by the third week of December 2003, Kit Symons was in temporary charge following the resignation of Steve Kember, and the Palace were near the bottom of Division 1, with only two wins since the end of August. That week, Palace lost 1-3 to Crewe Alexandra at Selhurst Park, a result which pleased my work colleagues but not me and Palace were facing the distinct possibility of relegation at the end of the season.

Following this latest disaster, the club turned to yet another manager for salvation and this time it seemed to work. Ian Dowie had previously cut his managerial teeth at cash-strapped Oldham, but after not being paid for a period, he decided to move on and Selhurst Park was where he came to. The effects were immediate, and by the time the Palace lined up for the Valentines Day fixture at home to Stoke, they had lost just one game since the end of December 2003 and the play-offs were becoming a distinct possibility.

I recall my friends and I were in the Main Stand for this game, and right from the start, we were treated to goals, and not just one or two either. The prolific goal-scorer Andy Johnson led the way with a first-half hat-trick including two penalties, and Stoke responded with two goals of their own, and by the time half time was reached, the score was an unusual and breathless 4-2. If it was thought that the second half might be an anti-climax, it certainly proved otherwise, and by the time the final whistle was blown, the Palace had won 6-3, only the second time I had seen my team score six goals in a League game. The hunt for a play-off place continued.

Result CPFC 6 Stoke City 3, attendance 16,700, referee Rob Styles

Postscript

After the game, we headed back to Croydon for a meal before dispersing. We alighted on a very nice small restaurant near the town centre, and it was only when we went in and saw the roses on the table that we remembered it was Valentines Day and the restaurant was obviously geared up for a romantic evening for its customers. We decided to stay and I have to say that the staff treated us royally, despite our lack of romantic connections, and we enjoyed a really good evening there. I think this photo may have been of a different meal, but I know the footballing sentiment on the table amused us.

Game 30 - Crewe Alexandra v CPFC, 24th April 2004, Division 1

The play-off push continued, and by the time the Palace lined up for the return fixture against Crewe in April 2004, they had put together fifteen wins in twenty-one games, and a play-off spot was becoming more and more likely, subject of course to a win at Gresty Road. No wonder this was a key fixture which I wanted to attend.

In normal circumstances, I would have got a ticket for the Main Stand with the home fans. However, my friend and longstanding Palace fan Philip wanted to see the game as well, and so we decided to go in the Away Stand, curiously named the Whitby Ice Cream Van Stand. It was with some trepidation that we made our way into the Stand. It was a very warm April afternoon and a large following from South London was expected to fill the small 1,700 capacity Stand. The sun was beating on our faces from the outset, and it promised to be a long, hot and very noisy afternoon under the low roof of the Stand.

Of course, the Palace had to win to keep alive their hopes of making the play-offs, and when ace striker Andy Johnson scored not once but twice in the first half against a struggling home side, it seemed that they had done enough to do just that. However, the Alex were made of sterner stuff under Dario Gradi, and football legend and later England international Dean Ashton quickly reduced the arrears after the interval. If there was trepidation in the Away Stand, it did not last long as Andy Johnson completed his hat-trick from the penalty spot and we could start to think of the play-offs and possible promotion, a seemingly impossible thought just four months previously. However, back came Crewe again and a goal from another Alex legend, Kenny Lunt, meant a nervy last fifteen minutes was in store for the Palace fans. Then, with just a minute or so remaining - a terrible mistake in the Palace defence and there was a Crewe player with the goal gaping to make it 3-3 and dash our hopes of a play-off spot. We held our breath as he put the ball….. wide of the goal and into the home fans at the Gresty Road end. We howled with derision. 3-2 was how it ended a minute or two later and the Palace charge towards promotion under Ian Dowie was still on. However, it had been a close call and the Palace players and management knew it. It only remained for me to hear the congratulations from my work colleagues the following Monday which I recall came through gritted teeth!

Result Crewe Alexandra 2 CPFC 3, attendance 8,100, referee Keith Hill

Postscript

It seemed that the Palace team wanted to keep their long-suffering fans on tenterhooks a bit longer after the Crewe game. A win at home to Walsall was achieved courtesy of a follow-up to a late and controversial Andy Johnson penalty which consigned the West Midlands side to relegation, with only a point now needed at Coventry in the final game of the season to secure a play-off spot. Amazingly, Palace managed to lose the game 1-2 and thus needed Wigan to drop points against West Ham on the same afternoon to maintain their hopes of promotion. However, Wigan were leading 1-0 as the game entered the last minute and all hopes for the Palace seemed to be over for another season. But then West Ham equalised. Cue bedlam at Coventry and sighs of relief from among the Palace faithful. Promotion was now becoming much more than a distant dream.

I did not see either of the epic semi-finals against Sunderland, but I do recall peering through a pub window to see a late and controversial Darren Powell header take the second leg to extra time, Palace having been reduced to ten men earlier in the game. I got home in time to hear most of extra time and the penalty shoot-out on the radio. Never have I listened to a radio more intently as I did that evening as the shoot-out went first one way and then the other until finally Michael Hughes buried his effort in the net to send the Palace through to the play-off final. It may have been sometime after 10pm, but I was in dire need of a stiff drink to calm my nerves!

A familiar sight for Crewe Alexandra fans, with a panoramic view from the Main Stand looking towards the small Ice Cream Van Stand which we occupied in April 2004

Game 31 - CPFC v West Ham United, 29th May 2004, Division 1 Play-off Final

We had reached the Play-off Final, something which we would scarcely have thought possible after the defeat at home to Crewe Alexandra just five months previously. But who would we be facing in the Final? Why, West Ham of course, the same West Ham that had got us there in the first place when they equalised late on at Wigan and who had beaten Ipswich in the semi-final to reach the Final. It could not have been better scripted. And, although our London neighbours had finished one point and two places above us in the final League table, there was a quiet air of confidence in the Palace camp as the game approached. We might have just squeaked into the play-offs, but we were not about to let the prize slip from our grasp now. And the financial rewards for gaining a place in the Premiership would mean a probable end to the financial issues which had blighted the Palace over previous years. No wonder the game was labelled the 'hundred-million-pound' game.

Of course my friends and I had to be there, but where would be heading to see the game? By now, the Final was a one-off game rather than two legs and was normally played at Wembley. However, that stadium was in the middle of a complete rebuild and so it was to the Millenium Stadium in Cardiff that we headed on a sunny, warm Saturday morning. The three coach train from Crewe to the Welsh capital was crowded for the two-hour journey, and - as in 1991 on the M40 – it was noticeable how many 'ex-pat' football fans from both sides were heading from the Northwest to the Welsh capital for the game. However, it was all very good-natured, and we could only hope that it would stay that way on the journey home.

I had not previously been to the Millenium Stadium and I was immediately struck by how modern it all was, and this was perhaps unsurprising in view of its name which it had been given at its opening just five years previously. Our seats were high up at the Palace end and I was reminded of visits to Newcastle United where the away fans were (and still are) housed high up in a stand and it takes an age and great effort to climb the stairs to get there.

West Ham were the favourites for the game, but the Palace quickly made it clear that they were not going to yield easily to their more illustrious London opponents. The first half was perhaps shaded by West Ham, but Palace came out all guns blazing in the second half and took the game to The Hammers, attacking the goal at our end. And then, just after the hour, Andy Johnson set off on one of his typical mazy runs before unleashing a left foot shot across the goal towards the far corner. The West Ham goalie dived full length but could only parry the ball and there was Palace captain, Neil Shipperley to score the simplest of tap-ins to give his side the lead. Was he offside? No VAR of course and all eyes were momentarily on the linesman on the far side, but he was not flagging, and Shipperley had obviously timed his follow-up just right. The Palace fans around and below us went wild. The final half-hour of the game was predictably filled with tension, but I cannot recall the Palace ever being in real danger of relinquishing their precious lead and the final whistle was the cue for wild celebrations on and off the pitch. As the legendary TV commentator Brian Moore put it, Palace had gone from relegation candidates to promotion reality in just five months and all under the stewardship of Ian Dowie. No wonder his name was chanted by the Palace fans at the end.

The evening journey back north was predictably long, but fortunately not beset by problems on the train, and I think maybe the fans from one side of London were too tired celebrating a famous victory and from the other side too shell-shocked to care. For the Palace, another season in the top-flight beckoned, but could they make it stick this time?

Result CPFC 1 West Ham United 0, attendance 72,500, referee Graham Poll.

The squads for the Play-off Final at Cardiff in May 2004

Nationwide FOOTBALL LEAGUE

DIVISION ONE PLAY-OFF FINAL

CRYSTAL PALACE

2	Curtis FLEMING
3	Danny GRANVILLE
4	Danny BUTTERFIELD
5	Kit SYMONS
6	Tony POPOVIC
8	Andrew JOHNSON
9	Dougie FREEDMAN
10	Shaun DERRY
11	Neil SHIPPERLEY
12	Jamie SMITH
13	Cedric BERTHELIN (GK)
14	Ben WATSON
15	Aki RIIHILAHTI
16	Tommy BLACK
17	Michael HUGHES
18	Gary BORROWDALE
21	Julian GRAY
22	Wayne ROUTLEDGE
24	Mikele LEIGERTWOOD
27	Nico VAESEN (GK)
28	Tom SOARES
29	Gavin HEEROO
30	Lance CRONIN (GK)
32	Darren POWELL
35	Andrew McCORMACK
36	Andrew TIPPING
43	Sam TOGWELL

WEST HAM UNITED

2	Tomas REPKA
3	Rufus BREVETT
4	Don HUTCHISON
5	Robert LEE
6	Michael CARRICK
7	Christian DAILLY
8	David CONNOLLY
10	Marlon HAREWOOD
11	Steve LOMAS
12	Matthew ETHERINGTON
14	Wayne QUINN
15	Anton FERDINAND
16	Kevin HORLOCK
17	Hayden MULLINS
19	Adam NOWLAND
20	Nigel REO-COKER
21	Richard GARCIA
22	Andy MELVILLE
25	Bobby ZAMORA
26	Jobi McANUFF
29	Brian DEANE
30	Pavel SRNICEK (GK)
31	David FORDE (GK)
32	Stephen BYWATER (GK)
35	Chris COHEN

OFFICIALS

REFEREE	ASSISTANT REFEREES	FOURTH OFFICIAL
G Poll (Hertfordshire)	R Lewis (Shropshire) T Massey (Cheshire)	N Barry (Lincolnshire)

Game 32 - Sheffield Wednesday v CPFC, 22nd March 2008, Championship

The answer to that last question was a sad 'No' and, once again, the Palace fell from the top-flight after only one season. It was not for want of trying and I saw them gain a precious late-season point - 0-0 - at Newcastle when the defence stood firm and Andy Johnson cut a lonely figure up front. However, one point proved to be too little as a late Charlton equaliser in the final game consigned the Palace to the newly named Championship, just one point and one place below West Bromwich Albion who were saved, and with a better goal difference. It was a cruel way to end the season.

Ian Dowie continued as manager in 2005/6, but after guiding them to a Play-off semi-final and a defeat over two legs against Watford, he left under difficult circumstances and his place was taken by Palace 'Old Boy' Peter Taylor. Peter's tenure of office was neither particularly successful nor a complete failure, but by the time of my next game in March 2008, his place as manager had been taken by Neil Warnock.

Easter 2008 was very early and, with family connections in Sheffield, it made sense to pay them a visit over the weekend and see my favourite team in action at Hillsborough at the same time. Easter Saturday was particularly cold and as we made our way to the ground, there was snow in the air as well as on the hills around the city. It was not an issue in the ground and the travelling faithful were soon warmed up with a goal at our end from Matt Lawrence. However, The Owls hit back and, by midway through the second half, they had a 2-1 lead. That is when the fun started as the snow which had been threatening for a while suddenly started to descend in great blobs, quickly covering the pitch and players. Christmas 1968 came to mind, and I half-wondered whether I would once again be seeing a Palace game abandoned. Calls for the referee to abandon the game in fact began to cry out at our end as Palace continued to chase the game to no apparent avail, but as the game entered its final minutes, it became clear that it would be played to a conclusion, come-what-may, and we could only hope that the Palace would find an equaliser from somewhere before the end. But where, and would we actually see it at the far end as the by-now heavy and continuous snow swirled around in the gathering gloom of a dark March afternoon? Then, as the game moved into added time, there was an audible groan from the Wednesday end. But why? The answer was not long coming as the Palace players emerged from the snowy gloom clearly celebrating a goal. Who scored it? Nobody at our end had a clue, but the record showed it was Ben Watson who applied the finishing touch following a Palace corner. 2-2 was how it ended, and it was time to battle the elements as we made our way back towards the snow-covered city centre. It was an afternoon to remember for the many Palace fans who made the journey to Sheffield on that oh-so-cold, snowy Easter Saturday afternoon in March 2008.

Result Sheffield Wednesday 2 CPFC 2, attendance 19,900, referee Russell Booth

Postscript

Palace reached the Play-off semi-finals again, thanks to a last-day 3-0 win over Burnley at Selhurst Park, but that was as good as it got, and defeats in both legs against Bristol City consigned them to another season in the Championship.

Game 33 - Blackpool v CPFC, 25th October 2008, Championship

Despite the disappointing Play-off semi-final defeat the previous season, Neil Warnock continued as manager in 2008/9. By then, Crewe Alexandra had long dropped out of the Championship and so my friends and I made plans to see the Palace play at Blackpool in October 2008, a convenient meet-up location from our homes dotted around the UK. I had previously lived at Blackpool in the 1990s and had seen the home side play a few times whilst I was there, notably an entertaining FA Cup tie against high-flying QPR (which they drew), and a key relegation match against Orient which they won to stay up. I had also seen the Palace come from behind to beat Blackpool 2-1 at Bloomfield Road in the FA Cup in January 2003, and I was looking for something similar or better in 2008.

Two 'flies in the ointment' became evident before the match. One was the warning that because of major redevelopment work that was being carried out at Bloomfield Road, the away fans could be expected to be housed in temporary and open terracing, and the other was the weather forecast which was dire, with high winds and heavy rain predicted throughout the afternoon. A not unusual autumn afternoon in Blackpool in other words and, to be honest, I was rather hoping the game might be postponed.

As I travelled up the motorway to Blackpool, the weather was not actually that bad, and I began to wonder whether the rain might stay away until after the end of the match. Faint hope, as by the time I joined my friends in a local pub, the rain was coming horizontally off the Irish Sea in a near gale-force wind. We wondered whether to stay in the warmth of the pub, but we had made the effort to get to Blackpool, and my friend Martin had thoughtfully provided some bin liners for temporary cover, so off we went to brave the elements in what was rapidly becoming a thoroughly unpleasant afternoon.

If we had hoped that the Blackpool FC authorities might take pity on the away fans and house them in one of the new stands, given that a large crowd was not expected, these hopes were quickly dashed as the temporary and open terracing came into view once we entered the stadium. However, it was approaching 3pm and there was nothing for it but to don our bin liners and find seats next to the pitch-side wall which might at least provide some protection from the elements. It was clear that the Palace fans were not a happy bunch, and I was reminded of a similar situation at a game I attended at Newcastle some years previously when the Palace Chairman had joined the away fans on the open temporary terracing as a protest rather than sitting in the Directors Box.

Once it started, the game itself was quite entertaining, and goals from Hill and Beattie helped the Palace to a 2-2 draw. In other circumstances, we would probably have been quite happy as we left the ground, but this was no ordinary afternoon, the bin liners had only worked so far, and it was time to hurry to our overnight hotel to get changed and dry out. At Sheffield Wednesday, it had been snow, and at Blackpool, it was rain and wind. What next, I wondered? I later noted with grim satisfaction that the attendance at Blackpool was comfortably the lowest of the season for a League match involving the Palace, and I have to say I was not surprised.

Result Blackpool 2 CPFC 2, attendance 7,600, referee Anthony Taylor

Postscript

The game was refereed by Anthony Taylor, then quite inexperienced at that level and with a full mop of hair, and I thought he had a good game in difficult conditions. As with Mike Dean in 2000, we were to see a lot more of Anthony over the years and, in the view of many, he is still one of the top two referees active on the Premier League in England.

I was to see Palace play at Blackpool again a few years later when they managed to concede two late goals to lose 1-2. By then though, the redevelopment work had been completed and the accommodation for the away fans was quite acceptable. However, memories of that awful afternoon in October 2008 live on to this day.

Even the bin-liners failed to keep the elements out on that stormy afternoon in Blackpool!

Game 34 - CPFC v Scunthorpe, 12th Sept 2009, Championship

At the end of the 2008/9 season, Palace found themselves just below halfway in the Championship and, with Neil Warnock remaining at the club to give them some continuity in those turbulent times at Selhurst Park, there must have been some hope that their fortunes on the pitch would take a turn for the better in the following season. However, reality soon kicked in and, by the time they started their sixth League game against Scunthorpe, they had just one win to their name and were already close to the bottom of the table.

My three longstanding school and Palace friends, Martin, Philip, Andy and I were all born in the last few months of the 1940s, and so we all had a 'big' birthday to celebrate in late 2009, and where better to celebrate it than with a game at Selhurst Park. On this occasion, we decided to 'splash-the-cash' and purchase a hospitality package in what is now called Speroni's Restaurant in the Main Stand. It seemed odd to be turning up at Selhurst Park three hours before kick-off, with hardly anyone around, but we were soon seated in the restaurant ready to enjoy our lunch followed by seats in the Main Stand for the game plus drinks at half time and at the end. I have to say the meal was very good, we met former players who came to the restaurant to 'meet-and-greet', and we even had time to go on the pitch and have our photographs taken before we went to our seats for the game.

All well so far, but what about the game? Well, let us just say that the Palace had an off day, so 'off' that by the time the final whistle blew, the score was 0-4, and Palace were starting to get nervous about their future in the Championship. It was a day of celebration for us, but a pity about the result.

Result CPFC 0 Scunthorpe 4, attendance 12,900, referee Grant Hegley

At least we were still smiling before the kick off!

The terraces in the background were never like this in 1962!

Postscript

Neil Warnock continued as manager until March 2010 but was then replaced on a temporary basis by Paul Hart. I saw them gain a creditable point at Derby in the penultimate away game of the season and could have seen them play the final game of the season at Sheffield Wednesday but decided against it. This was partly because the game was being shown live on the BBC and partly because I didn't think my nerves would stand it, Palace needing a draw and Wednesday a win from this 'show-down' game to send the other side down to League 1. In the event, Palace got their point in a 2-2 draw and it was Wednesday who went down as a result. Who knows what would have happened if Wednesday had snatched a win at the death and sent the Palace down, and we could only hope that things would get better the following season on and off the pitch. And Scunthorpe? Well, after finishing one place above the Palace at the end of the 2009/10 season, they began a decline which took them out of the Football League and ultimately into the National League North from where they have just been promoted. I saw them play at Crewe Alexandra in League 2 before they were relegated from the Football League and felt sorry for the club and their long-suffering fans. But such can be the changing fortunes of being and supporting a football club at that level, as the Palace and their fans were soon to find out.

Game 35 - CPFC v Derby, 17th November 2012, Championship

The managerial merry-go-round continued, with George Burley and Dougie Freedman coming and going, and by the time the team lined up for the game against Derby in November 2012, Ian Holloway was in charge at Selhurst Park. And, perhaps rather surprisingly in view of the comings-and-goings, Palace were going great-guns in the Championship and were on an unbeaten run in the league stretching over fourteen matches.

I am sure my friends and I could have found seats in the Arthur Wait Stand for this game, but once again we reached into our pockets for the hospitality package in the club restaurant. As part of the lunch deal, there was a raffle with prizes such as signed footballs and shirts on offer. Tickets were a rather eye-watering £10 each and I think the four of us bought one ticket each and hoped that one of us at least might strike lucky. I recall that I was in the toilet when the draw was made and, when I got back, it was clear that something was up. The first prize had not been claimed, and my friends' tickets had only just missed out. Had I got the winning ticket? You bet I had, and my friends and I could now look forward to yet another hospitality package for four, including seats close to the Directors Box, for a future game at Selhurst Park. It was clearly £10 well spent. But where would the Palace be when we next visited them, bearing in mind that they were doing so well in the Championship? Could it possibly be in the Premier League and would the Palace honour the raffle prize if they had been promoted by then? More on that shortly.

And the game against Derby? Well, unlike Scunthorpe, Palace did us proud that afternoon and a 3-0 win was thoroughly deserved. Small wonder that we were a happy bunch as we left the ground and wended our way homewards.

Result CPFC 3 Derby 0, attendance 16,200, referee Fred Graham.

Game 36 - CPFC v Watford, 27th May 2013, Championship Play-off Final

The unbeaten run came to an end just a week later at Leeds, but the push for a return to the Premier League continued. However, a poor run-in meant that Palace had to settle for fifth place in the Championship and a place in the play-offs. After Brighton had come to Selhurst Park and held the home team to a 0-0 draw in the semi-final first leg, few would have given Palace much hope of getting through to the Final. However, the Palace of Ian Holloway were made of sterner stuff, and a 2-0 win at Brighton in the second leg meant that it would be the South Londoners who would be going to Wembley rather than their arch-rivals. And of course, my friends and I wanted to be there to see them play and hopefully defeat their opponents – Watford - in the Final.

I had been to Wembley stadium twice since the redevelopment had been completed in 2007. In August 2012, I had been lucky enough to get a ticket for the Olympic Men's Football Final between Mexico and Brazil which Mexico surprisingly won 2-1; and in early April 2013, my friend Philip and I enjoyed watching my adopted home-town team, Crewe Alexandra beat Southend 2-0 in the Johnson Paint Trophy Final, with Philip becoming an honorary Crewe fan for the day. The stadium was very modern, a bit like the Millenium Stadium in Cardiff, and completely unlike the Wembley that I remembered from the early 1960s when bench seats had no backs and wellies were recommended for visits to the Gents, amongst other things! Having found our seats towards the Palace end, we sat back and enjoyed the pre-match show and then it was time for the £100 million game to get underway, Palace v Watford for a place in the Premier League.

If we thought we were in for a goal-fest, we were to be sorely disappointed as neither side seemed able to break the other down. Palace may have had their former legend Wilf Zaha playing whilst he was back on loan from Manchester United, but thirty-goal ace Glenn

Murray was missing injured, and it showed. Watford were poor but Deeney almost won it for them, only to be thwarted by a fine save by another Palace legend, Julian Speroni. So it was stalemate at ninety minutes, with the tension of extra time and possible penalties to come.

The blank scoreline continued until the 105th minute whereupon Wilf tricked a Watford player into a rash challenge and went down in a heap in the area, with the referee immediately pointing to the spot. Penalty! Would Wilf take the penalty? No, as ace penalty-taker, former Watford player and football veteran Kevin Phillips stepped forward and buried the ball in the net. Cue an explosion of joy and noise at our end. However, there were still fifteen minutes left to play and Watford were not about to give up on their dreams without a fight, and in the very last minute, it seemed that they had equalised until Joel Ward somehow managed to get back and scramble the ball off the line. The final whistle was not long coming and we could start the celebrations in earnest. After eight consecutive seasons, Palace were back in the Premier League, and this time, we could only hope that their stay would be longer than one season. It was the end of an exhausting day, on and off the pitch.

Result CPFC 1 Watford 0, attendance 82,000, referee Martin Atkinson

Postscript

I had now seen Palace play in three Division 2 / Championship Play-off Finals in three separate locations, and they had won them all. A lucky mascot perhaps?

Wembley, here we come!

We are going up!

Game 37 - CPFC v West Bromwich Albion, 8th February 2014, Premier League

Would the Palace stay up this time? Well, their first season back in the Premier League started badly, so badly in fact that in late October 2013, Ian Holloway resigned and was replaced the following month by Tony Pullis, and after that, results began to pick up.

For some reason, probably logistics, my friends and I had been unable to take up my raffle prize prior to the end of the 2012/3 season, and now of course, there were other factors to add to the equation, notably capacity crowds for most of the fixtures, our availability from around the UK, and a regular changing of dates and times of games, often late in the day, to suit the demands of TV. Eventually, we agreed on the game against relegation-threatened West Bromwich Albion on a Saturday afternoon in February 2014 and I contacted the club, hoping they would honour the prize for four people over a year after my ticket had been drawn out first. And, rather to my surprise, they did.

The day proved very similar to the previous occasion we had attended for a hospitality package, and I noted, with rather a smile, that the first prize in the raffle was now down to two seats in the Main Stand and nothing more. Needless to say, we did not win. We were unable to go pitch-side this time, perhaps understandably and, when we came to access our seats, we found they were right at the back of the Main Stand and with a quite restricted view of play. However, we were grateful to the club for honouring the prize, which must have been worth several hundred pounds.

By half time, Palace were 2-0 up, with goals from Ince and Ledley, and cruising to a third home win on the bounce against struggling opponents. It was then back to the Restaurant for coffee, and by the time we returned to our seats for the second half, the game was underway again. The atmosphere seemed strangely muted, but we could not see the screen or score from where we were seated, and it was only a few minutes later that we were told that WBA had scored in the first minute of the half whilst we were finishing our drinks. 2-1, game on it seemed. However, if nerves were setting in on and off the pitch, they did not last long, and a Chamakh penalty with twenty minutes to go confirmed Palace's rise up the table, which eventually saw them in eleventh place. Palace had survived in the Premier League at last. We were a happy bunch as we made our way homewards at the end of a long but successful day, and all for £10.

Result CPFC 3 WBA 1, attendance 24,500, referee Chris Foy

Crystal Palace Football Club

Registered Office: CPFC Limited, Selhurst Park, London, SE25 6PU Company No. 07270793

Crystal Palace F.C.
Selhurst Park Stadium,
London, SE25 6PU

Tel: +44 (0)20 8768 6000
Fax: +44 (0)20 8771 5311
www.cpfc.co.uk

CONGRATULATIONS!!

You have won....

4 x Executive Packages in Speroni's Restaurant

at a CPFC Home Championship Fixture in Season 2013/2014 of your choice*

Includes Director's Box Seating and Lunch

** B or C grade games only, Subject to availability.*

We were in the Premier League by then so definitely a bargain at £10!

Game 38 – CPFC v AFC Bournemouth, 9th December 2017, Premier League

Palace may have survived, but the managerial merry-go-round continued, with Neil Warnock, Alan Pardew and Sam Allardyce all in charge over the next three seasons. Alan was perhaps the most successful of these, and it was he who took the Palace to Wembley in 2016 for their second FA Cup Final appearance where, once again, they lost to Manchester United. However, by the start of the 2017/8 season, Palace's fifth consecutive season in the Premier League, the Dutchman Frank de Boer was in charge at Selhurst Park.

The season started disastrously, and after four games, Palace had no points and no goals to their name. After the last of these games, at Burnley which my friends and I attended, Frank was sacked and the club looked to a local man with boyhood connections at Selhurst Park, former England manager Roy Hodgson, for salvation.

If there were thoughts that the popular Roy would bring immediate results to the club, these were quickly dashed with three defeats on the spin, ten goals conceded and still no points or goals on the board. However, a shock win, 2-1, in a London derby against Chelsea got them going at last and, although there was to be only one more win before December 2017, a few draws meant that the team had not been left completely behind in the Premier League by the time they lined up for the six-pointer home game against AFC Bournemouth on 9th December. It was a game which my friends and I were determined to attend.

As I indicated in the postscript to Game 1, my first at Selhurst Park, Bournemouth did not become 'AFC Bournemouth' until 1971, and I hope I will offend no-one if I continue to call them 'Bournemouth' in this book. The rise of the club was little short of meteoric, with three promotions in six years taking them to the Premier League in 2014/5.

For some reason, probably to do with getting tickets together, I found myself in the Main Stand for the Bournemouth game, with my friends located opposite in the Arthur Wait Stand. It was Jermain Defoe who gave the visitors an early lead, only for the Palace to hit back with two goals before half time, the second coming from a Milivojevic penalty following a foul on Wilf Zaha. There was still time for one more goal in the first half as the veteran Defoe showed that he had lost none of his skills with a superb dipping half-volley which completely out-foxed Julian Speroni in the Palace goal. 2-2 was how the score remained in the second half and into the last few minutes of the game, whereupon a Palace player went down in the area and, after some thought, the referee pointed to the spot. Penalty, cue bedlam. For the second time that afternoon, ace penalty taker Luka Milivojevic stepped forward to take the kick and likely give the home team three priceless points in their battle against relegation. But hold on a moment. What was going on? It seemed that another Palace player, Christian Benteke, wanted to take the penalty and was not about to allow anyone else to get in the way. The big-money signing had failed to open his scoring account that season and now it seemed that he wanted to put this right with a crucial penalty kick. It was a high-risk gamble, and it certainly did not meet with approval, least of all from Roy Hodgson who was standing on the touchline barking instructions for Christian to hand the ball over and Luka to take the kick. It was all to no avail as Christian shuffled up to take the kick without any great conviction and then put a weak shot far too close to the Bournemouth goalie who saved with ease. The reaction on and off the field was instant and universal, and the look on Roy's face said it all. 2-2 was how it finished and Palace remained at the bottom of the Premier League. I suspect words were said in the Palace dressing room after the game which could certainly not be printed in this book.

Result CPFC 2 Bournemouth 2, attendance 24,800, referee Kevin Friend

Postscript

Palace did not have to wait long for the win which they should have secured against Bournemouth, and victories over Watford and Leicester before Christmas, plus two further wins in January 2018 took them up the table and towards safety. And by the time my friends and I returned to Selhurst Park for the penultimate home game of the season against Leicester, the job was almost done. The visitors were but a shadow of the side that won the Premier League title just a couple of seasons previously, and a 5-0 scoreline was a fair reflection of play that afternoon. The game would have been soon forgotten, but for a late Palace substitution and an even later penalty which was buried by the substitute for the home team's final goal. And who was the substitute? I will leave you to guess, but let us just say that all was clearly forgiven as the Palace eased towards eleventh place at the season end.

Game 39 – CPFC v Bournemouth, 3rd December 2019, Premier League

Bournemouth were to feature again when we attended the final game of the 2018/9 season at Selhurst Park which the Palace won 5-3. It was ninety minutes of pure entertainment between two teams with nothing to worry about in terms of relegation. The game was the last for home team legend Julian Speroni before he retired, with emotional farewells and ovations on and off the pitch at the final whistle. It was also the last game for referee Roger East, and I was pleased that he was included in the handshakes and embraces at the end of his last game at the top level. It was that type of game.

Roy Hodgson was in charge throughout the season, and he continued in post the following season when our thoughts turned again to 'big' birthdays and the possibility of celebrating them with a game at Selhurst Park. But which game? The demands of the TV companies continued to disrupt our well-laid plans, often at short notice, but eventually we alighted on a Tuesday evening game at Selhurst Park in December 2019. And who should be the opponents? Why, Bournemouth of course.

On this occasion we plumped for the hospitality package in the Legends Restaurant which was (and is) located over the Whitehorse Lane Stand and offered panoramic balcony seating for the game. I have to say the buffet meal was very good, former players came in to 'meet-and-greet', and then it was time to take our seats for the game, and yes, the view from our open balcony seats was panoramic.

If we were looking for pure entertainment again, we were to be disappointed as both teams struggled for an opening, let alone a goal. Then, after twenty minutes, a high challenge in midfield by Mamadou Sakho and Palace were down to ten men for the remaining seventy minutes. The decision looked correct from where we were sitting. Despite their numerical advantage, Bournemouth never really worried the home team and the first half ended goalless, and it was time to go back indoors for some suitable refreshment on a cold December evening.

The second half continued in the same pattern and my thoughts turned to my first game at Selhurst Park which of course ended 0-0 against Bournemouth. However, with just fifteen minutes remaining, Palace substitute Jeffrey Schlupp burst through the middle to score with a powerful shot from the edge of the area, and there was much jubilation on the balcony, with one rather drunken fellow having to be pulled back from the low balcony railing as he threatened to launch himself towards almost certain oblivion in the Stand below.

1-0 was how it ended and Palace had reached the exalted heights of fifth place in the Premier League. It was the perfect end to an evening of celebrations for our big birthdays.

Result CPFC 1 Bournemouth 0, attendance 23,500, referee Anthony Taylor

Postscript

If Palace had aspirations of Europe the following season, they quickly dwindled, with just one win between the Bournemouth game and late February 2020. By the beginning of March 2020, the threat of Covid was beginning to trouble the nation and a win against Watford on 7th March proved to be the last game for three months for the Palace and the last game of the season at which fans were present. Following the announcement of the first pandemic lockdown, the Premier League season was extended to late July and when Palace played their much-delayed return fixture against Bournemouth on 20th June, the official attendance was '0', as it was at all other Premier League grounds. Palace won that one 2-0 to complete the double over Bournemouth, but that was as good as it got and, by the time the season finally ended with a 1-1 draw against Spurs, again with an attendance of '0', Palace were in fourteenth place. It was a sad way to end a promising season.

Our 70th birthday celebrations in the Legends Restaurant in Dec 2019

The view from the balcony was good

Game 40 – CPFC v Aston Villa, 27th Nov 2021, Premier League

Palace continued in the Premier League the following season - 2020/1 - with Roy Hodgson as manager throughout the campaign. Once again the crowds were absent due to the pandemic, and it was only at the end of the season, and games against Arsenal and Liverpool in May 2021, that some spectators were allowed to attend. At the end of the season, with Palace safe in fourteenth place, Roy decided to leave and his place as manager was taken by the Frenchman, Patrick Vieira. Roy had worked wonders at Selhurst Park since being appointed in September 2017, but now he felt it was time in his 70s to take a step back from football, and there was clearly a lot of respect for that decision. Would we be seeing him again? I think we know the answer to that one, but I will come back to it shortly.

The start of the 2021/2 season was promising and included victories over Spurs and Manchester City; and by the time my friends and I returned to Selhurst Park, after an absence of almost two years, for the game against Aston Villa, thoughts were already turning to Europe, with nothing short of a victory against Villa expected.

There was certainly a 'fly in the ointment' so far as the Palace were concerned and that was the new Villa manager - one Steven Gerrard – who, having been an all-time great player at Liverpool and then a successful manager at Rangers for three years, had now moved back south to manage the West Midlands side. Early play bore all the hallmarks of Steven, with the Villa getting stuck in from the first whistle and taking a deserved lead in the fifteenth minute. It was not pretty to watch, but mixing it and not allowing Palace to play open football was clearly part of the Gerrard game plan and it seemed to be working as the match progressed through to the interval and into the second half with Villa still in the lead. The referee – Michael Salisbury, son of former Football League referee Graham Salisbury – was in charge of his first Premier League game, and at times, his lack of top-flight experience showed. I wondered whether Gerrard had planned for that as well. Probably. Then, midway through the second half, a flashpoint as a Palace player was taken out crudely near the halfway line and a red card was produced. 11 v 10 and hope for the Palace at last. But hold on a moment, the Video Assistant Referee (or VAR as they are more commonly known) wanted Michael to have another look at the incident on the screen and, for the first time, I was about to witness a VAR intervention live. Rather surprisingly in my view, the screen was situated in front of the Arthur Wait Stand, perhaps to prevent the managers taking a sly look from their dugouts and, less surprisingly, having looked at the screen, Michael accepted the advice of the VAR, who I think may have been Michael Oliver, and changed the card from red to yellow. The Palace management, players and fans were not happy, but later viewings on TV suggested that the yellow card was correct. 1-0 was the score until the last few minutes of the game, whereupon Villa scored a second goal and Palace replied with a consolation goal. 2-1 to the Villa was how it finished and our return to Selhurst Park had ended in disappointment.

Result CPFC 1 Aston Villa 2, attendance 25,200, referee Michael Salisbury

Postscript

Patrick Vieira continued in post until the end of the season which saw Palace in a respectable twelfth place in the Premier League. However, the season was noted more for Palace's FA cup run which took them to the semi-finals at Wembley and defeat to Chelsea.

Patrick was still in charge the following season – 2022/3 - but was sacked in March 2023 after a poor set of results, and who should the Palace turn to for salvation? Step forward Roy Hodgson. If the move to bring Roy out of retirement in his mid-70s seemed strange to say the least, it also proved to be an inspired one as Palace moved up the table to twelfth place at the end of the campaign.

Roy was in post again the following season – 2023/4 - but after a similarly poor set of results and complaints about the lack of entertainment in Palace games, he left in February 2024. It was a sad way for Roy's stellar career in football management to come to an end, and fans from many clubs and countries had cause to be grateful to him, but it was now time to move on and Palace turned once again to foreign soils, and the Austrian, Oliver Glasner, to be their new manager.

And that is how it is today in 2025. Palace have completed their twelfth consecutive season in the Premier League and who would have thought that when they came up via the play-offs in 2013. Oliver Glasner has continued as manager and, after starting badly, results picked up and Palace ended up in a respectable twelfth place. Not for the first time, mighty Manchester United were beaten at Old Trafford, something which I would never have thought possible in my early days supporting the Palace in the 1960s. And the FA Cup? Well, clearly I need to say something about the team's recent achievements in the FA Cup, but if I may, I will leave this to another chapter.

Where did I feature in all this and why do I appear to be concluding my story with a humdrum Premier League game played almost four years ago and with no obvious 'wow' factor apart perhaps from a first glimpse of VAR. Well, I have to admit that the game against Villa was the last time I saw Palace in action live. There are various reasons for this, including the regular changes of dates and times of fixtures to accommodate TV, often at short notice, difficulties in getting group tickets for games, and logistical difficulties in coming together at Selhurst Park from our locations around the UK. Before the pandemic, my friends and I regularly met up at Burnley and Newcastle to see our favourite team in action, but even this has tailed off since 2020, partly due to us all getting older and unwilling to stand for ninety minutes and more because fans in front of us refuse to sit down. Moan over! So, we have been left to watch our team on television and look out for the results when we are out and about. I am sure we shall need to have one last 'hurrah' at Selhurst Park, perhaps via a hospitality package once again, before we get too old to enjoy it, and hopefully it will be in the Premier League which is where the Palace deserve to be.

I actually have two more games to report on, but as the first does not directly involve the Palace, and I was not present for the second, I will not include them in my games with a 'wow' factor. I invite you to read on.

Arsenal v Aston Villa, 30th May 2015, FA Cup Final

You may be wondering whether I have taken leave of my senses in my old age. Why have I included a game which did not involve the Palace, and have I perhaps got the wrong year for the FA Cup Final and should be referring to the Final in 2016 when of course the Palace were involved?

Well, yes and no. Yes, there is a link between the 2015 Final and Palace and No, I have not taken leave of my senses and got the wrong year. Puzzled? Let me take you back to Game 5, Palace v Leeds in the FA Cup in March 1965, a game which I desperately wanted to attend but for which I failed to get a ticket, much to my frustration. Now, fast-forward to early 2015 when I happened to be thumbing through some media and spotted a story-writing competition run by the BBC in conjunction with their 'Songs of Praise' programme. The competition organisers were looking for short stories relating to each of the sixty four teams in the third round of the FA Cup that year, which of course included Crystal Palace, with the winners for each club representing their team at Wembley on FA Cup Final day and joining a 'Songs of Praise Choir' to sing the traditional Cup Final hymn, 'Abide with Me', on the pitch before the game. I pondered for a while. As a keen football fan, story writer and amateur singer, I wanted to take part, but what could I write about? Then the frustrations of the Leeds game fifty years before came to mind and I started to write… and write, in fact so many words came pouring out that the 'delete' button then came to the fore, much to my annoyance. Eventually, I arrived at a story of five hundred words, much of which has been detailed in Game 5, and I pressed the 'send' button and thought nothing more of it.

The deadline came and went without comment, but a couple of weeks later, I arrived home to find the BBC had been in touch and would be phoning later. I began to wonder and yes, when they got back in touch, it was to say that I was the winner of the competition for the Palace and would be representing them at Wembley on Cup Final day. Was I pleased? You bet I was.

At the time, I recall Palace were still in the FA Cup, having overcome Dover and Southampton in the third and fourth rounds, and my friends and I rather hoped that they would overcome mighty Liverpool in the fifth round and go all the way to Wembley where my friends could see me in action before the game. Sadly, this did not happen.

If I had thought that it would be a matter of turning up at Wembley on the morning of the match, singing a couple of verses of Abide with Me, and then watching the match from the stands, these thoughts were quickly dispelled. This was a two-day operation with hotel accommodation provided by the BBC for a couple of nights near Wembley.

There was a good deal of preparation involved before the day, and mine included purchasing the latest Palace home shirt from the club shop. I was tempted to look for a 1965 shirt, but did not think that it would go down well with the organisers or club. Not being local meant that any publicity had to be run from afar and in my case, I have to admit it was patchy.

Friday 29th May and, right on time, sixty-four of us turned up at Wembley, suitcases in hand, ready for a busy two days ahead. All the big clubs were represented, and it was good to see some of the smaller clubs there including Dover, Southport and Marine. We were a motley crew, with ages ranging from 18 to 100 (the Newcastle representative was a few weeks away from his telegram), men and women, and all with the shirts of their favourite teams, making for a colourful sight.

Our base for the next two days was a press room at the stadium, and it was here that we were introduced to our music director, the genial Steve Thompson, who was clearly a football fan as well as a very able musician. It was then time for our first rendering of ‘Abide with Me’, and it quickly became clear that we had not been selected for our singing abilities. As a keen singer, I thought of trying to harmonise the hymn and singing the bass part, but I quickly thought better of it.

The rest of the day was spent at the stadium, rehearsing the hymn over-and-over again, in the press room to begin with and then on the hallowed turf itself. Later in the day, we were introduced to the earpieces which would be an essential tool on the day and we quickly got used to the '1-2-3' in the ear before we began to sing Abide with Me for what seemed to be the umpteenth time. It was a long day and, just before we thought it was all over, there came a surprise for some of us as a BBC London TV news programme wanted to see the local club representatives live on air and hear us sing Abide with Me. Frantic calls to friends and families ensued as we tried to get the programme recorded and, shortly before 7pm that evening, a group of us from the London clubs appeared live on air, suitably adorned in our club shirts. I recall the Chelsea and Millwall representatives being interviewed and we then played out the programme with a hearty rendering of Abide with Me, with Steve conducting off-camera. By all accounts, our contribution was a success and it came at the end of a very long day.

Saturday 30th May 2015 – Cup Final day - dawned warm and sunny, thank goodness, and by 9am, we were back at the stadium and on the pitch ready for the final rehearsals. By this time, the stadium was a hive of activity and I noted Dan Walker presenting BBC Breakfast further down the pitch. And within an hour, we had sung Abide with Me one more time to end the breakfast programme live on BBC1.

Until now, rehearsals had been accompanied by recorded music, but later in the morning, we were introduced to the Band of the Brigade of Gurkhas who would be accompanying us in the actual performance that afternoon. And since the Band were to be situated a considerable distance away from us, the reason for our earpieces became evident as, without this tool, we would not be able to hear them and they would not be able to hear us. It took a bit of getting used to, but it seemed to work.

Back in the press room, we were introduced to some of the guests who were attending the Final. The fine Welsh singer, Aled Jones, was one of them, and Alfie Boe, who would be singing with us that afternoon, was another. I had mixed views about having a professional singer with us, but Alfie was a friendly person and I was pleased that I was able to meet him. The surprise came later on when who should come through the door but one Roy Hodgson. At the time, Roy was the England manager, although whether he was there to view potential England talent or just as a guest, I do not know. He was a very friendly man and he was another I was pleased to have met. I was of course to see much more of him in later years.

With kick off at the later time of 17.30, there was still time to wander around our 'safe' area under the main stadium and, in my case, I was able to take a photo of the door to the referee's dressing room. I was rather hoping I might see the match referee, Jon Moss, and have a word with him, but I suspect he was elsewhere in the stadium at the time and the opportunity passed. It must have been a great day for him and his team as much as it was for us. A view through the security doors confirmed that the stadium was filling up nicely, with noise coming from all sides of the ground.

At last it was time to line up in twos, nerves a-jangling, ready to march out onto the pitch for our big moment. Predictably, the line was led by the Arsenal and Villa fans, and we came out via a tunnel at the Villa end of the ground rather than the players' tunnel which had been re-sited at the halfway line during the redevelopment of the stadium a few years earlier. The sight and sound which greeted us was incredible, with around 90,000 fans chanting away and the music accompanying a gymnastics display booming around the ground. We took our places near the halfway line, Alfie Boe came to the front with Steve Thompson, and we awaited the familiar '1-2-3' in our earpieces, with the Ghurkhas striking up the famous tune to 'Abide with Me' after '3'. By then, we had all learnt the two verses of the hymn by heart, but to ease forgetful memories, the stadium authorities had thoughtfully provided the words on screens around the stadium, and we were able to sing the verses with gusto and without looking down at the words in our programmes. High up in the gantry, the BBC were beaming pictures of the choir across the world to watching millions, and all around us, cameras clicked away recording the occasion for posterity. Who would have thought that I, a keen but not particularly able amateur singer, should one day perform in front of a live audience of 90,000 and a worldwide TV audience of many millions.

And then it was all over and we marched off the pitch as quickly as we had entered it, with a roar shortly afterwards announcing the arrival of the teams on the pitch for the match. It only remained for us to take our places for the game, in my case with a group at the Arsenal end and enjoy the proceedings. And at the final whistle, the Arsenal fans were still chanting following a fairly comfortable 4-0 win.

I hope I have not bored you with an additional game which did not directly involve the Palace, but you will see that I have many memories of a wonderful occasion in my footballing life, and all because I failed to get a ticket for a Palace game fifty years previously.

64 teams were represented at Wembley ...

... including Cardiff, Palace and Ipswich ...

... and Roy Hodgson and Aled Jones were welcome guests

Crystal Palace v Manchester City, FA Cup Final, 17th May 2025

In all honesty, I could not have allowed publication of this book without mention of arguably Palace's finest hour, their FA Cup Final triumph in May 2025, and this despite the fact that I was not actually at Wembley to see them do it.

There were good reasons for my absence from both the Semi-final and Final at Wembley which I shall not go into, suffice to say that I was with the Palace every step of the way, in the case of the Semi-final v Villa, from far away. However, members of my family plus my friend Martin and his son Andrew were there on both occasions, and I am grateful to them all for keeping me supplied with video clips and photos from the games which I have been able to enjoy at home.

For me, the FA Cup Final has to be watched on the BBC, and although much of the pre-match ritual has changed over the years, it was good to hear the band strike up 'Abide with Me' before the teams emerged from the tunnel. My mind was immediately taken back ten years and my own involvement in this annual ritual, and I have to say I felt a bit emotional as the fans joined with the professional singer to sing the famous football hymn.

Introductions to Royalty and National Anthem over, it was time for action and, unsurprisingly, Manchester City took the game to the Palace from the start, and it seemed that a repeat of their 6-0 triumph over Watford in the 2019 Final could be on the cards. And then what did the Palace do? Well of course they went up the other end and scored a fine team goal finished off by Eze in the 16th minute. It was not just at Wembley that Palace fans went wild. But could they hold on to the lead for another 75 minutes or more, or crumble as they had done in a recent League game against City?

And then, controversy, as Palace goalie Dean Henderson handled the ball outside the penalty area to nick it from the foot of the advancing Haaland. Nothing was given by the referee, Stuart Attwell, but the VAR quickly intervened and it seemed that England international and Palace favourite Dean Henderson might be heading for an early bath. However, after some delay, the VAR sided with Attwell and the decision was made that Henderson had not denied Haaland a clear goal-scoring opportunity. The City management and fans were clearly not happy, but we were. Were Stuart and the VAR right? Probably not, according to the Rate the Ref website, but it was not clear-cut by any means and I, for one, was glad that the game continued 11 v 11.

Did it matter? Well, yes, it certainly did as City player Silva went down in the Palace penalty area following a tackle from Mitchell, and after some thought, Stuart Attwell pointed to the spot. Penalty! Soft? Yes, definitely, but it was not a decision that the VAR was ever likely to recommend overturning, and Haaland had the ball in his hands ready to try and draw City level. But hold on a minute, what was happening? There was Haaland handing the ball over to Marmoush to take the penalty. If ever there was a Christian Benteke moment, this was it. Countless breaths must have been held as Marmoush stepped forward and blazed the ball towards Henderson's right, only for the Palace goalie to guess correctly and save the shot and follow-up. It was a magnificent double save from the England international and the Palace fans went wild with delight behind Henderson's goal. What the reaction was at the other end was not clear, and to think, Henderson might not have been there to save the penalty.

If the first half was entertaining, the second was nerve-wracking in the extreme as the Palace tried to hang on to their lead, knowing that if City equalised, they would almost certainly go on to win. After an hour, apparent relief as Munoz scored a second for the Palace, only for the goal to be chalked off by the VAR as Sarr had unintentionally played the ball in an offside position in the build-up. A frustrating but correct decision.

The game seemed to go on and on, and I found myself going back and forth to the loo in the frequent breaks for substitutions and the like. It was probably as well that I was not at Wembley! City favourite and England international Phil Foden came on as a substitute and surely he would work his magic to conjure up one chance to take the game into extra time. But no, there was no way through, and Henderson was playing out of his skin. How much added time would there be? '10' (minutes) was what was on the fourth official's board and the groans from the Palace end could clearly be heard on the TV. Yet more defending to do as City mounted increasingly desperate attacks, yet more saves for Henderson to make, and then it was all over, the final whistle blew, and Palace had won the FA Cup for the first time. It was not just the players and fans at Wembley who were in tears at the end. The wait of 119 years for a major trophy was over at last.

I was pleased that all the players in the squad went up with manager Oliver Glasner to receive their medals from Prince William, and it was good that unused substitute Joel Ward, the last surviving member of the 2016 FA Cup Final squad, who was retiring after the 2025 Final, was on hand to receive the Cup with captain Marc Guehi. What if Joel had not been on hand to make his last-ditch goal-line clearance in the final moments of the Play-off Final against Watford in 2013? We shall never know of course, but we were glad that Joel's many years of service at Selhurst Park were rewarded in this way. And the BBC 'Man of the Match'? I will say no more.

I was also pleased that a number of Palace faces from the past were there to see the game and trophy presentation, including Steve Coppell, Alan Smith and Roy Hodgson. It was fitting that they should be there on the club's greatest day.

And a word too for Palace Co-owner and Chairman, Stephen Parish. He had been instrumental in saving the club from administration in 2010 and had been in charge ever since as the club rose from seeming oblivion to the Premier League and the FA Cup. It must have been a proud day for him.

Finally, let us not forget the thousands of fans who supported the club through thick and thin and who helped to make the Wembley Final a special day in the club's history. Their support was fantastic, and as

Steve Parish said afterwards, "the win was for the supporters, we owe them a trophy, this is for all the people who believed in us".

The next few pages are given over to photos from Cup Final day and the Victory Parade around and at Selhurst Park. The first is of me preparing for the Final at home, and then photos from family members, Colin, Mary and Hannah, and friend Martin and his son Andy. I am grateful to them for allowing me to use these photos to bring back memories of Palace's greatest achievement. Sorry folks, nothing terribly professional about them, but I hope you enjoy seeing them as much as I did.

TDK

EMIRATES FA CUP 2025
CRYSTAL PALACE F.C.

CRYSTAL PALACE
CUP FINAL
2025

Crystal Palace FC, aka The Eagles and South London's No 1

FA Cup Winners 2025

No wonder I'm feeling …… GLAD ALL OVER!

CONCLUSION

The best and worst of it

I have now reached the end of my memories, but before I blow the final whistle, I want to have a look back at the best and worst of my time supporting the Palace, using the forty games with a 'wow' factor as a yardstick.

The best game – there are several contenders here, but for me the best game I attended was at Wrexham (game 20) in May 1977. It had everything, plenty of goals and entertainment throughout, and a dramatic ending which saw the Palace take a giant step towards promotion to Division 2. For games at Selhurst Park, the win over mighty Nottingham Forest in February 1965 (game 4) and the promotion clincher against Fulham in April 1969 (game 12) take some beating. Moving into the present millennium, the 6-3 win over Stoke in February 2004 (game 29) comes out on top for goals and entertainment, with the game against Bournemouth (game 38) in December 2017, including its dramatic ending, coming in a close second.

The worst game – this was undoubtedly game 11 - Palace v Middlesbrough – in April 1969. I have attended many games at different grounds over the years, and I can say with certainty that I have never seen a game as dull as this one.

The best goal – I am sure this has to be Peter Burridge volleying the Palace back into the lead in the game against mighty Nottingham Forest (game 4) in 1965. OK, the ball could well have ended up somewhere along Whitehorse Road rather than the back of the net, but it did not and memories of this 'goal-in-a-hundred' thus live on to this day.

The game with the biggest 'wow' factor – there are several contenders including, from my early days, Palace v Blackpool in 1970 (game 16) when the referee failed to spot Gerry Queen's right hook, and Palace v

Fulham in October 1978 (game 21) when the referee decided to take the time from the stadium clock, although of course I never saw the repercussions of his crass decision. And the dramatic ending to the game against Bournemouth in 2017 (game 38), involving Christian Benteke, means this game takes top spot in the present millennium.

The best Palace team – I am not into Palace 'all-time-greats', but here are a few of the players I feel have contributed most over the past sixty years. In goal, I must include John Jackson, along with Nigel Martyn and Julian Speroni. In front of them in defence, I am certain that a place needs to be found for the craggy Scot, John McCormick, who made almost two hundred appearances for the Palace and was an ever-present during the promotion season of 1968/9. In midfield, Jim Cannon gets my vote, having played a record 660 games for the club over fifteen seasons. Moving forward, Andy Johnson comes out on top, with his 74 goals in 140 appearances contributing in no small measure to the Palace being where they are now. Mention too for Cliff Jackson and Bobby Woodruff from the 1960s and 1970s, along with Ian Wright, Mark Bright, Glen Murray and Wilf Zaha from more recent times. I salute them all, along with all the players from the present squad.

The best Palace manager – I am sure you will understand my reasons for nominating Bert Head and Roy Hodgson for this award, with honourable mentions too for Terry Venables, Steve Coppell, Ian Dowie, Ian Holloway and of course Oliver Glasner. Again, I salute them all.

The best referee – in a straw-poll on the Rate the Ref website, Joe Worrall from Warrington came out on top, and quite right too in my view. However, although I saw Joe in action on several occasions until his retirement in 1995, this was not in any of the forty games with a 'wow' factor, and so I have put him aside. Roger Kirkpatrick was undoubtedly the most entertaining referee in the forty games, but the best referee was Roger's Leicester colleague, Peter Reeves, for his calm, assured handling of the 'winner-takes-all game' (game 20) at Wrexham in 1977. Peter was always one of the best referees on the list, and his appointment to the 1979 League Cup Final was well-deserved. Special mention too for Mike Dean (game 28), who I always enjoyed watching in more recent times, and his refereeing of the Palace crunch game at Sheffield Wednesday in May 2010 was in my view top-notch.

When I lined up outside the Whitehorse Lane end of Selhurst Park in April 1962, I never for a moment thought that I would be doing the same sixty years later and writing about my experiences. The question has sometimes been asked of me, is the game better or worse than in the 'good-old-days'? Well, it has certainly changed over the past sixty years. It is a lot quicker and more skilful, and players and referees are a lot fitter than most of their earlier counterparts. More emphasis has been placed on cracking down on serious foul play, with the disgraceful behaviour in the FA Cup Final replay between Chelsea and Leeds in 1970 being used as a catalyst for change, and quite right too in my view. VAR and goal-line technology have helped to reduce controversy at the top levels, although VAR is still questionable at times in my view. Facilities at grounds are undoubtedly better although those at Selhurst Park are still far from perfect. Yet, in some senses, the game has become too clinical and too professional, with Premier League clubs in particular being required to pander to the demands of media and worldwide TV audiences rather than ordinary fans. And at times, I yearn for the days when I could turn up at Selhurst Park, or other grounds where the Palace were playing, at 2.30pm on a Saturday afternoon, pay my money and sit and enjoy the game with my friends. It does still happen at Crewe Alexandra, but not at Premier League grounds. Does that answer the question? Probably not, but then I am not sure what the answer is anyway, and I will leave it at that.

The final whistle

Two final sightings of ‘Crystal Palace’, but where is the first one? George Street, Croydon perhaps (see the road sign)? No, over 500 miles away from Croydon in NW Scotland. Funny how far the Palace reputation travels. I was amused anyway!

No doubts about this one! And with thanks to Martin, Philip and Andy for making it all possible.

"They think it's all over, it is now", and with acknowledgements to the late great Kenneth Wolstenholme, I conclude my memories of the past sixty years and more of supporting Crystal Palace Football Club. Thank you for reading my book, and I hope you have enjoyed it.